MW00675954

PranOorja

Raho positive hamesha!

Yog Guru
DR. SURAKSHIT GOSWAMI

Pran Oorja

First published in 2009

by

Bennett, Coleman & Co., Ltd.
7, Bahadur Shah Zafar Marg
New Delhi-110002

Editing, Design & Production: Times Group Books
Printed and Bound by : Nutech Photolithographers

ISBN 978-81-89906-41-2

Price: Rs.350

*G*od has bestowed on humanity innumerable virtues. But many a person lets himself or herself remain sadly confined to "I am". The Ego is thus a restriction, a self-demarcated boundary blocking a person's spiritual progress. Our venerable rishis of yore have long described various practices of yoga to inculcate a better sense of broadmindedness - an 'It's me' feeling.

Indeed, the essence of life is to remain steadfast to one's true-self. When a practitioner of yoga is in this state, all his virtues become evident and he becomes an embodiment of love, knowledge and bliss.

Yoga is an Indian system of keeping the body fit in every way – physically, mentally, emotionally and spiritually. Though there is no prescribed age for beginning the practice of yoga, an early start would be more beneficial. Yoga gives an enormous fillip to our dormant faculties and may take us to new heights of self-realisation and achievement.

It is becoming increasingly difficult for our youth to make time for exercise today. Although people do want to stay fit they are unable to arrange a slot for yoga in their busy schedule. Stress diminishes the body's life-force day-by-day. This makes us prone to various diseases. It is, therefore, important that our youth become conscious of these problems and turn to yoga for much more than just sorting these out.

Keeping this in mind, Dr. Surakshit Goswami has described in detail two processes of yoga in this book that are especially designed to give maximum benefit in a short time.

I hope the yoga exercises, as described in this book, would rejuvenate our youth and allow them to scale whatever heights they desire in a long, healthy and fruitful life.

Blessings!!

Indu Jai

Indu Jain
Chairman, Times Group

Contents

Preface

Yoga is a philosophy, a science and an art. Yoga is also a therapy. It is India's ancient scientific method of keeping the body and mind fit. Its practice instigates positive attitude in the practitioner, which augments creativity and enhances the frontiers of thought. Yoga is meant for everybody. It's neither bound by the shackles of caste and creed nor by age. The only prerequisite is to have faith and a firm belief in its benefits. And follow a regular, daily regime of yoga practice.

Owing to our busy, hectic schedules, we are unable to give enough thought to our health. Our fast-track lifestyle invites innumerable physical and psychological ailments — our meal-times and sleep habits have been disturbed; physical labour has decreased and inner thoughts are suffused with negativity. All these have resulted in an increase in tension and depression. Largely due to these factors a person starts to age before time. A bit of work exhausts and saps charm off our faces. We tend to get irritated even by trifles, thus reducing our intellectual capabilities. Creativity and Positivity get diminished. All these act as a stumbling block in our way to progress.

Modern lifestyle has resulted in an increased number of cases of obesity, stress, hypertension, diabetes, deformity of backbone etc. In such a situation, a person, even if he/she wants to do something for his physical and mental wellbeing, is at loss. They just don't know what to do —whether they should join a gym, go for walks or practice yoga. Again, what should be the duration of the workout, how to get maximum benefit from the minimum time put in for the purpose, whether there are any side effects or not, etc. All these lead to procrastination.

While some people, notwithstanding their hectic schedule, are conscious about their health and try to remain fit, a majority of them remain negligent towards it. Keeping these predicaments in mind, we have prepared an exercise regime called **Pran Oorja Yog** after several years of research. This exercise takes only 30 minutes. If a person can manage to take an half-hour slot out of his busy schedule, he/she will be able to keep diseases at bay and remain energetic throughout the day. Pran Oorja Yog can also help in curing several diseases which have already attacked the body. It is highly effective in keeping a person agile and youthful for a long time.

Besides the 30-minute Pran Oorja Yog, this book also describes the three-minute **Pran Oorja Kriya**. One's mind attains peace and attentiveness by practicing this *kriya*. This *kriya* is a panacea for mental problems. It can be practiced by all, anywhere and anytime.

This book also contains valuable information related to diet and a daily routine for a healthy life.

This book was made possible due to the blessings of the Almighty. I was simply the medium; the real motivating factors were my elders and other righteous people. For this I offer my sincere regard and gratitude to my spiritual guru, my father Pandit Narendra Goswami and mother Shrimati Lakshmi Devi, and Professor Ishwar Bharadwaj ji, Chairman, Department of Yoga, Gurukul Kangri University, Haridwar. Simultaneously, I am also grateful to all those who, directly or indirectly, are related to the publication of this book.

Dr. Surakshit Goswami
March, 2009

Celebrating Life with Yoga

Life is a celebration and should continue to be so for as long as we live. With the passage of time, it should, in fact, become more pleasurable. But seldom do we perceive life as being joyous. It is essential to remember that this celebration is not an external phenomenon but an internal one. In fact, it is a state of mind where everything appears blissful.

However, the journey of life is not always smooth. Our fickle nature makes us act according to our whims and fancies. And while flitting from one thought to the next, our mind often becomes attached to unnecessary things.

One often wonders why the mind is so fickle. The reason is simple enough. We are so influenced by physical desires that our mind is always wavering and is in turmoil. The mind is happy as long as things happen in accordance with its desires. The moment events take a sudden turn and our wishes are not fulfilled, it becomes sad and perturbed. As a result, it alternates between *sukh* (happiness) and *dukh* (agony). We must remember that true happiness and peace do not lie in material things. They only deceive the mind and prevent it from remaining calm and focused. If you are unduly attached to material objects, even after spending a lifetime searching for happiness in the external world, peace and happiness will continue to elude you.

The state of our mind controls our physical health. A mind that wanders gets disturbed easily and causes tension and despair, which, in turn, can lead to sickness and ill health. In such a condition, it is futile to take steps to regain physical health while neglecting the mind. Instead, we should understand and control our mind to prevent diseases. This is how we can make our life a celebration.

The question that then arises is -- how does one understand the mind? How does one rein it in? The solution lies in delving deep into the mind and establishing a communion with one's inner self. In the process, one becomes an embodiment of love, compassion, equality and bliss. This is the state of dhyaan (meditation). And this is the beginning of yoga.

The discipline of yoga is a precious heritage of the Indian culture. For ages, irrespective of considerations of religion, race, caste and sect, yoga has been practised to heal physical and mental ailments of human beings. One cannot attain the knowledge of yoga easily. To master yoga, you must aim to lead an ideal way of life and seek the blessings of a *guru* (master). You should practise yoga regularly, with complete dedication to keep your body, sense organs, mind and life force free of ailments. As a result of this, you will move swiftly on the road to spirituality and realize your inner self.

According to Maharshi Patanjali — who was eminent in the field of yoga and had compiled the *Yog Sutra* — the basis of yoga lies in curbing certain traits of the mind, like ego and attachment, in order to help individuals break away from their worldly shackles. He calls this "yogaschittavrittanirodhaha". Our mind is constantly wandering either in the past or in the future owing to a chain of thoughts (*vritti*s) that cloud the mind. These thoughts — influenced by the environment we live in and arising because of certain characteristics that we inherit — influence our responses to the material world, giving rise to *sanskaara* (traits). Maharshi Patanjali has classified these chains of *vritti*s into five categories — Pramaan, Viparyaya, Vikalpa, Nidra and Smriti.

A *saadhak* (practitioner of yoga) remains in a pure and free state of mind. He gladly accepts the *praarabdh karm* (inevitable actions) that are destined for him. All *sanskaara* (accumulated acts of the previous life) are destroyed and no action occurs owing to a sense of non-attachment.

The practice of yoga expands your horizon and spurs you on to positive thoughts. You are filled with feelings of affection and compassion towards everyone and all your confusion and doubts are cleared. Your face radiates happiness as you develop integrity of mind. As you continue to practise yoga, even adverse conditions fail to perturb you. No wonder then, that yoga makes your entire life a celebration.

VARIOUS FORMS OF YOGA

Various forms of yoga have been mentioned in Indian classical texts. Prominent branches of yoga are **Rajyog**, **Gyanyog**, **Bhaktiyog**, **Kriyayog**, **Asthangyog** and **Hathyog**. Different people benefit from different branches of yoga as each one of us is different — the *punya* (good deeds) that we have accumulated, our *sanskaara*, our states of mind and the guide under whom we practise, are supposedly different. Whichever branch of yoga you choose to practise, you will experience a pleasurable feeling of liberation and lead a happy, peaceful and healthy life. Two main branches of yoga — **Asthangyog** and Hathyog — are described in this book. Importantly, **Pran Oorja Yog**, which has been conceived and developed after years of research to combat problems related to current lifestyle, has been described in detail.

Asthangyog

This is a simple form of yoga. A *grahastha* (householder) too can reach the higher state of yoga by following the path prescribed in Asthangyog. It is an important training regime, details of which have been comprehensively described by Maharshi Patanjali in his *sutras*. The eight parts of Asthangyog are **Yam, Niyam, Aasan, Pranayam, Pratyaahaar, Dhaarna, Dhyaan** and **Samaadhi**.

Yamaniyamaasanpranaayaamapraharadharanaa dhyaanasamadhayoshtvangaani

(*Yog Sutra*, 2/29)

YAM

Maharshi Patanjali speaks about five *yam* — **Ahimsa, Satya, Asteya, Brahmacharya** and **Aparigraha**.

Ahimsasatyamsteyabrahmacharyaaparigraha Yamaha

(*Yog Sutra*, 2/30)

1. **Ahimsa:** To hurt anyone, either physically or mentally, using one's limbs, speech or mind under the influence of anger or passion is *himsa* (violence). Simply put, **ahimsa** (non-violence) involves love and compassion towards all living beings. *Ahimsa* has been considered to be the best *yam*.

The rules of the other four *yam*, i.e. satya, asteya, brahmacharya and aparigraha are followed only to reinforce ahimsa.

2. **Satya: Satya** is to describe something exactly the way it has been seen, heard and comprehended. In the *Mahabharata*, *satya* that is beneficial to human beings is elevated to a higher plane.

3. **Asteya:** To acquire something illegally or by theft, against the tenets of *dharma*, is known as *steya*. **Asteya** means neither being attracted to the possessions of others nor nursing a desire to possess them.

4. **Brahmacharya:** To keep a control over one's physical desires is called **brahmacharya**. Compared to other organs of the body, the reproductive organ increases physical desires the most. Hence, the emphasis is on keeping a restraint on one's reproductive organs.

5. **Aparigraha:** The accumulation of objects that one desires is known as *parigraha*, whereas non-acceptance of these objects is called **aparigraha**. It is not considered desirable to amass material wealth in excess of one's requirement. *Aparigraha* is what one should aim for.

NIYAM

Maharshi Patanjali has described five *niyam* (rules) in the *Yog Sutra* — **Shauch, Santosh, Tapa, Svaadhyaya** and **Ishwara Pranidhan.**

Shauchasanthoshatapaha
Svadhyaeshwarapranidhanani niyamahaa
(*Yog Sutra*, 2/32)

1. **Shauch:** There are two kinds of *shauch* (purification) — external and internal.

   ■ **External Shauch:** External purification constitutes cleaning one's body, clothes and the place of *saadhna* with soil, soap and water; one's body can be kept pure by restricting oneself to a simple diet and remaining active by practising yoga regularly.

   ■ **Internal Shauch:** The process of internal purification involves renunciation of one's negative attitude and habits by adopting a positive way of life. It includes adherence to friendship, compassion, joyfulness and neutrality, and shunning away negativity and hatred.

2. **Santosh:** Being satisfied with whatever one has instead of hankering for more material wealth is called **santosh** (contentment). When the desire for material wealth dwindles, the *saadhak*'s mind soars high. *Santosh* leads to happiness, whereas *asantosh* (discontentment) leads to suffering.

3. **Tapa:** One should have control over one's body, pran (life force), organs and mind just as an expert rider controls a wild horse. This is known as **tapa**. It involves restraining the outward flow of energy from one's body, accumulating it and giving it an upward mobility. Tapa, without which yoga is incomplete and imperfect, enables one to brave hunger, thirst, heat, cold and remain calm in adverse conditions.

4. **Svaadhyaya:** In **svaadhyaya**, the practitioner studies and contemplates about his inner self. Chanting the sacred *Aum* and studying enlightening scriptures like *The Bhagavad Gita*, the *vedas* and the *upanishad*s aid in Svaadhyaya. Here, the emphasis is on *sva* or self and the practitioner's aim is to understand his inner self and his innermost thoughts.

5. **Ishwara Pranidhan:** The feeling of respect, love, submission and devotion towards God is **Ishwara Pranidhan**. It is also the act of dedicating our karma, body and mind to God.

AASAN

Sthirasukhmaasanam
(*Yog Sutra*, 2/46)

According to Maharshi Patanjali, the position in which the body can remain motionless or still for a stipulated period of time is known as **Aasan**. In the above *sutra*, Patanjali has defined aasan and described its recommended duration and inherent advantages. One should remain in a aasan position for as long as one's body is comfortable and is in a state of bliss. But one should change the aasan when one starts alternating between stability and instability, joy and sorrow. It is not easy to keep one's body still as one tends to move one's hands and legs frequently. Aasans, when practised, keep the body and mind stable and joyful. They liberate us from confusion and duality and help us reach the peak of *saadhna*. However, Maharshi Patanjali is silent about the number of aasans in his *sutras*.

PRANAYAM

Praanasya aayamah — the word Pranayam is derived from two separate words, pran and *ayam*. **Pran** is the breath or life force without which no one can survive. **Ayam** means stabilizing or expanding the pran. The process of inhalation and exhalation begins at the time of birth and ends with death. One can live without food and water for a certain period of time, but pran is essential for survival. Pranayam can help one control his breath or life force. Maharshi Patanjali says the following about Pranayam:

Tasmin sati shvaasprashvaasayorgativichhedah praanayamah

(*Yog Sutra*, 2/49)

By practising Pranayam, one can gain control over the rhythm of inhalation and exhalation, choose to break the rhythm, and expand the life force in one's body. Maharshi Patanjali has described four kinds of Pranayam — Vaahyavritti, Aabhyantarvritti, Sthamhbavritti and Vaayabhyantara Vishayapekshi.

PRATYAHAR

According to Maharshi Patanjali, our *indriyan* (sensory organs) make our mind fickle. In a state of **Pratyahar**, these organs are brought under control and are, thereby, unable to have contact with the *chitt* (mind). Their attention shifts from outward objects and turns inwards. Hence, when the mind is in a thoughtless state, sense organs too get linked to the mind and get detached from the world.

DHAARNA

When, because of Pratyahar, the sense organs become introspective, they accept their objects by instinct. **Dhaarna** makes the mind concentrate inwards on a focal point (chakra). During Dhaarna, thoughts may develop in the mind and make it fickle. The training lies in ignoring such thoughts and effortlessly bringing back the mind to the same point.

Deshbandashchittasya dhaarnaa

(*Yog Sutra*, 3/1)

Dhaarna thus involves binding the mind to instinct at a particular place. Directing the attention of various sense organs away from objects of desire and concentrating the mind on various chakras in our body is called Dhaarna.

DHYAAN

According to Patanjali Yog, when your instinct stays continuously at the place where *dharma* resides, it is called **Dhyaan**.

Tatra pratyyaiktaanataa dhyaanam

(*Yog Sutra*, 3/2)

During Dhyaan, no object of desire pre-occupies the mind. Instead, instincts and thoughts that are related to a practitioner's concentration, flow like a steady stream of oil through his mind.

Dhyaan is a unique method of making the mind peaceful and inward looking. It removes negative feelings like desire, anger, ego, attachment and hatred and as a result, the practitioner can remain in tune with his inner self even while engaged in daily chores.

SAMAADHI

Samaadhi is the stage when Dhyaan attains maturity and becomes perfect. This stage is reached when the practitioner of Dhyaan focuses solely on his objective and his physical existence becomes immaterial.

Tadevaarthmatranirbhasam svarup shunyamiva samaadhih

(*Yog Sutra*, 3/3)

In a state of Dhyaan, the practitioner of Dhyaan (*dhyaataa*), the objective of Dhyaan (*dhyeya*) and Dhyaan intermingle to become one. It, then, becomes difficult to decipher the actual nature of *dhyeya*. But when dhyaan is intense and *dhyeya* becomes big, *dhyaataa* apparently transforms itself into *shunya* (egoless state) and perceives *dhyeya* as its own manifestation. In the state of Samaadhi, the nature of *dhyeya* becomes different from that of *dhyaataa* and dhyaan and is conspicuously felt in a cyclic manifestation of *dhyeya*. Just as salt becomes one with water when dissolved in it, similarly, the amalgamation of *aatman* (soul) and *mann* (mind) results in Samaadhi.

Two forms of Samaadhi have been mentioned: **Sampragyaat** (*savikalpa* or *sabeej*) **Samaadhi** and **Asampragyaat** (*nirvikalp* and *nirbeej*) **Samaadhi**.

Hathyog

Contrary to common perception, Hathyog is not yoga done under compulsion or force. The word *hath* is, of course, used for compulsion but when the word *yoga* is suffixed to it, the term acquires a spiritual meaning. The word *hath* is made up of two letters *ha*, i.e. Pingla Naadi or flow of pran through the right nostril and *th*, i.e. Idaa Naadi or flow of pran through the left nostril. Thus, as the life force enters into the channel of the spinal cord, the conjugation of hatha and yoga helps to awaken vital energies. Infinite mysteries of the physical body get revealed and the practitioner sets out on the path of spirituality. Practise Hathyog regularly to become immune to diseases. It is a scientific system of keeping the body, sense organs, mind and respiratory organs healthy. Though Hathyog has been mentioned in various texts, you can find its detailed description in *Hathyog Pradipika* and *Gherand Samhita*.

In *Gherand Samhita*, seven parts of Hathyog are mentioned: Shatkarm, Aasan, Mudra, Pratyaahaar, Pranayam, Dhyaan and Samaadhi.

SHATKARM

Shatkarm is essential for Hathyog. It purifies the body by releasing foreign elements, toxic material, faecal matter and impure air from the body, and prepares it for the practice of Hathyog. Shatkarm helps sharpen our mental faculties and keeps the body fit. Actually, the accumulation of impure material in our body is a disease in itself and Shatkarm helps to eradicate this disease. It also addresses irregularities of *vaat* (mind), *pitta* (bile) and *kapha* (cough).

Shatkarm includes six methods of purification of the body — Dhauti, Basti, Neti, Nauli, Traatak and Kapaalbhaati:

Dhautirbastistathha netirnauliki traatakam tathha
Kapaalbhaathishchaitaani shatakarmaani samaacharet
(*Gherand Samhita*, 1/12)

These methods are described here in detail on the basis of *Hathyog Pradipika* and *Gherand Samhita*.

1. **Dhauti:** According to *Gherand Samhita*, there are four types of **Dhauti** — Antardhauti, Dantadhauti, Hriddhauti and Moolshodhan. But *Hathyog Pradipika* describes only Vastradhauti.

    ■ **ANTARDHAUTI:** Antardhauti is of four types — Vaatsaar, Vaarisaar, Bahnisaar and Bahishkrit.

    i. **Vaatsaar:** Vaatsaar involves shaping one's mouth like the beak of a crow, i.e. joining the upper and lower lips to leave a small gap between the two lips and then inhaling air till the stomach feels full as if one has drunk water to the fill.

After that, the practitioner has to rotate the air inside his stomach and exhale it slowly through his nostrils. Vaatsaar Dhauti helps to cure ailments of the intestine and stomach and improves the appetite.

ii. **Vaarisaar or Shankha Prakshalan**: Vaarisaar Dhauti or Shankha Prakshalan is the process of cleaning the 32-ft-long intestine in our body. The term is derived from the fact that our intestine is shaped like a *shankh* (conch). This process cleans our body from inside, strengthens the intestine, improves the digestive system, and cures gastro-intestinal diseases. Here's how it should be performed:

Start the practice of yogaasan 8-10 days before you intend to do Shankha Prakshalan and the day before, eat food that is light and easy to digest. Before going to bed the previous night, eat about 50-100gm raisins cooked in milk. After relieving yourself in the morning, add some rock salt and lemon to a large pan containing hot water and drink a glass or two of this water while seated in Kaagaasan or Utkataasan position. Thereafter, practise five aasans — Taadaasan, Urdhvahastottanaasan, Katichakraasan, Tiryak Bhujangaasan and Udarakarshaasan — repeating each aasan five to six times. Repeat the complete cycle twice and drink a glass or two of water again. Those suffering from high blood pressure or skin diseases should add only lemon to the water, while those suffering from joint pain or knee pain should put only rock salt in the water. Do the five aasans as shown:

- **Taadaasan**: Stand erect and interlock fingers of both hands. Raise your hands above the head while inhaling air. Stretch your whole body and stand on your toes. Return to the normal position while exhaling. Repeat the process 5-6 times.

Taadaasan

- **Urdhvahastottanaasan**: Stand with your legs placed one foot apart. Interlock fingers of both hands and raise them while inhaling. Bend your waist and hands to the left side as far as possible. Return to the original position. Repeat the process on the right side. Do this aasan 5-6 times on each side.

Urdhvahastottanaasan

Katichakraasan

- **Katichakraasan**: Stand erect with your legs aligned to your chest and raise your hands in line with your shoulders. Next, inhale and take your hands towards the back from the left side while bending your waist to the left side. Then return to the original position while exhaling. Repeat this process on the right side. Do this aasan 5-6 times.

- **Tiryak Bhujangaasan**: Lie on your stomach. Put your palms near your shoulders so that your elbows are raised above the ground. Keeping

your feet apart, fold your feet and raise your toes. Now, raise your head and chest, supported by your hands, and bend towards the back and

Tiryak Bhujangaasan

inhale. Then try to look at your toes by turning your head over the left shoulder. Return to the original position while exhaling. Repeat the same process on the right side. Do this aasan 5-6 times.

- **Udarakarshaasan**: Squat on the floor, keeping your legs one foot apart and your palms on your knees. While inhaling, bring the left knee next to the right toe on the ground and press your stomach with the right knee. Look backwards by turning your

Udarakarshaasan

head to the right. Return to the original position after a while, exhaling. Do the same by changing the legs and the direction. Repeat 5-6 times.

Practise these five aasans in the above sequence. After this, drink 2-3 glasses of water. Drinking water after doing yoga will help you to relieve yourself easily. While passing stool, sit in the **Ashwini** position to contract and expand the anal muscles. After coming from the toilet, drink water again and repeat the aasan. You will again feel the urge to pass stool. Continue to drink water, do the aasan and relieve yourself. You can expect hard stool followed by semi-solid stool and then watery stool, depending on the number of times you drink water. After 8-10 times, even the flow of yellowish water will stop. Finally, the water you defecate will appear similar to that you had drunk.

Now, do some **Kunjal Kriya**. Drink four to six glasses of lukewarm water and then vomit it by inserting your finger into your mouth. After that, lie down in Shavaasan and cover your body with a sheet of cloth so that it is not exposed to air. After relaxing for half an hour, eat *khichdi* made with equal proportion of rice and moong dal (with husk). Add salt, turmeric powder and cumin seeds to the khichdi and avoid chillies. You can eat this *khichdi* with 50 to 100gm of ghee made from cow's milk. Ghee does not do any harm if taken after Shankha Prakshalan and has a beneficial effect on the intestine. After eating, you can do Yog Nidra. If you again feel hungry, eat *khichdi* but drink only lukewarm water in sips.

Precautions: After this exercise, you should avoid travelling, bathing, drinking cold water and inhaling cold draughts of air. Relax for the rest of the day and eat only *khichdi*. The intake of milk, curd, *mattha*, or any other milk product is strictly prohibited. Also, for 2-3 days, avoid the intake of any sour food or drink, oranges, grapes, tea, coffee, wine, cigarette, oily and spicy food. From the next day, take light and easy-to-digest meals because your digestive system has been completely cleansed. If you eat food that takes time to digest, you may suffer from fever, indigestion, constipation and bloating. Your intestine may also be weakened. However, children, persons who are weak and women who have recently given birth should not practise this *kriya*. You should avoid this exercise when the sky is overcast. While a healthy person may perform this *kriya* once in six months, those suffering from diabetes, chronic constipation, piles and obesity may do it every one or two months apart.

Advantages: Stool that has accumulated in the intestine for an extended period of time makes the blood impure and causes diseases. Therefore, the above *kriya* is effective in removing impurities and cleaning up the digestive system. It also cures stomach and digestion-related ailments like constipation, indigestion, loss of appetite, gas, obesity, piles and diabetes. This *kriya* provides relief from respiratory, gastric and skin diseases and helps cure headaches, appendicitis, mouth ulcers and hair-related disorders. It can regularise menstruation and eliminate joint pains and flatulence. By flushing out foreign elements and allowing the life force to start flowing throughout the body, this *kriya* will keep you healthy.

iii. **Bahnisaar:** After relieving yourself in the morning, either sit in the meditative posture or stand erect. Exhale forcefully and contract your abdomen in such a way that it touches your back, release it immediately. Repeat the process for as long as you can hold your breath. Practise this about a hundred times if possible. Bahnisaar increases your appetite by curing stomach diseases and helps to fight obesity and diabetes. It is also known as **Agnisaar kriya.**

iv. **Bahishkrit:** Do this exercise on an empty stomach in the morning. Shape your lips like the beak of a crow and take in air till your stomach is full. Retain this air inside your stomach for about one-and-a-half hours. Then release it from the anus. This *kriya* helps to purify blood vessels. **Precautions:** Do not practise this *kriya* till you have acquired the practice of retaining the life force for one-and-a-half hours. Otherwise, it can harm you.

■ **DANTDHAUTI:** It comprises four types — Dantmool, Jivhamool, Karnarandhra and Kapaalrandhra.

i. **Dantmool:** The process of cleaning the root of the teeth with catechu juice, clean and dry soil or any other medicine the first thing in the morning is known as Dantmool.

ii. **Jivhamool**: Cleaning the tongue by rubbing it with the index, middle and ring fingers in the morning on an empty stomach is called Jivhamool. This can gradually cure cough and phlegm.

iii. **Karnarandhra**: Cleaning the holes of the ears, using the index and ring fingers, is called Karnarandhra. You will feel a resonance while doing this.

iv. **Kapaalrandhra**: Cleaning the palate with the thumb and water each morning after leaving the bed is called Kapaalrandhra. This makes the blood vessels supple and improves the eyesight.

■ HRIDHHAUTHI: In this *kriya*, the stomach, or "the heart" as it is referred to, is cleansed in three ways — Dandhauti, Vamandhauti and Vaasdhauti.

i. **Dandhauti**: Drink as much water as you can early in the morning after answering nature's call. Then insert one end of a slim banana or turmeric stem in your mouth and let it go right down to your stomach. Hold the other end of this thin, stick-like object in your hand and try to rotate it inside your stomach. Then stand up, lean towards the front, take out the stem slowly and release water from the stomach. Dandhauti can cure stomach problems by expelling unhealthy phlegm and bile from the body.

Dandhauti is also called **Brahmadaataun**. This involves inserting one end of a piece of rope made of clean cloth inside the stomach after drinking water and then taking the water out of the stomach slowly using the portion of the rope that is outside. This *kriya* can also be performed with the help of a rubber tube.

ii. **Vamandhauti**: This involves drinking as much water as possible after a meal and vomiting it out along with the food you have eaten. This *kriya* can flush impure or poisoned food out of the body and cures ailments like cough, phlegm and bile. The *kriya* is also called **Baaghi** as tigers (*bagh* in Hindi) use the same process to expel spoilt flesh that they may have eaten.

iii. **Vaasdhauti/Vastradhauti**: After relieving yourself in the morning, sit in Kaagasan (squatting position) and insert into your mouth a piece of fine cloth, 15 hand-span long and 4-5 inches wide, which has been submerged in lukewarm water. Then start swallowing the cloth and stand up when only one hand-span of cloth is left outside. Rotate your abdomen and take out the cloth from the mouth. Follow it by Kunjal Kriya. Regular practice of this *kriya* cures diseases like fever, jaundice, leprosy, cough and bile.

■ MOOLSHODHAN (GANESH KRIYA): After relieving yourself in the morning, clean your anal region either with the root of a turmeric plant or with your middle finger and apply ghee or butter. This *kriya* cures indigestion and addresses sperm-related disorders and piles. By increasing your appetite, it improves your health.

Dhauti also includes Vaaridhauti, which is also known as Kunjar Karma or Gajakarni.

■ **Vaaridhauti (Kunjar Karma/Gajakarni):** Without eating or drinking anything in the morning, squat on the floor and fill your stomach with lukewarm water to which salt has been added. After that, stand up and lean forward; put two longer fingers of your right hand into your mouth and touch the base of your tongue. Vomit out the water. Press the left side of your stomach with the left hand and let more water come out. It removes cough, improves the appetite and helps fight obesity.

2. **Basti:** *Gherand Samhita* mentions two types of bastis — Jal Basti and Sthal Basti.

■ **Jal Basti:** Sit in **Utkataasan** in a large tub or pond. Constrict the anal region in such a way that water enters it, goes to the large intestine, and brings out the stool accumulated there from the anus. It addresses disorders related to phlegm, wind, bile and semen. Jal Basti provides relief from indigestion, gastric diseases, jaundice, cough and bile-related diseases. With improved appetite, your sense organs, mind and body too will become invigorated.

■ **Pawan Basti (Sthal Basti):** Lie in Paschimottanaasan position. Then contract and expand the anal region as in the Ashwini Mudra. By doing this, air will enter your body through the anus and come out through the same passage. This *kriya* is called Basti. It cures ailments of the stomach, flatulence, constipation and improves the appetite.

3. **Neti Karma:** These are of two types — Sutra Neti and Jal Neti.

■ **Sutra Neti:** According to the *Gherand Samhita*, this *kriya* should be done in the morning on an empty stomach using a specially knitted thread of about 15-20 inches in length. Insert one end of this thread into your "active nostril" and take it out from your mouth. This is called Neti Karma. According to *Hathyog Pradipika*, Neti Karma means inserting a soft thread into the nostril and taking it out from the mouth.

■ **Jal Neti:** This *kriya* is practised in the morning using a special jug or *lota* with a spout. Fill this jug with lukewarm water and add some salt in it. Then sit in **Kaagaasan**, put the jug's spout in the active nostril, bend your neck a little and breathe in and out through the mouth. Soon, water will start coming out from the other nostril. Repeat the process with the other nostril.

Kapaalshodhini Chaiv divyadristi Pradaayini Jatroodhrarajaataarogodyang netriraashu nihanti cha
(Hathyog Pradipika, 2/31)

This *sutra* means that Neti cleanses the head, removes impurities from the nose, ensures good eyesight and cures diseases of all organs that lie above the shoulders.

4. **Nauli Karma:** After relieving yourself in the morning, stand erect with some space between your two legs. Bend your knees slightly and place your hands on your thighs. Exhale the air

completely and squeeze in your stomach. Apply some pressure on your hands and bring out the central muscles of the stomach. Then, using your hands, rotate the central muscles of the stomach from left to right and vice versa. Called Nauli Karma or Nauli movement, it helps prevent diseases and improves the appetite.

5. **Traatak:** The word Traatak is made up of *tri* (three) and *taki bandhne* (to fix the gaze). In fact, the correct term is Tryaatak from *trivaaram aasmantat tankyati iti traatakam*. The act of concentrating his vision and mind on any one object by the *saadhak* is called Tryaatak. In due course, the word Tryaatak became Traatak. Here, *tri* doesn't signify three but instead continuity. When we look at an object, it is called **Ektak**. If

the same object is seen for some time, the action is called **Dvaatak**. And if we look at it without blinking our eyes for a longer time, it is called *Tryaatak* or Traatak. This *kriya* has been described in Hathyog to strengthen the eyes.

Traatak is of three types — Antahtraatak, Madhyatraatak and Bahyatraatak.

■ **ANTAHTRAATAK:** Antahtraatak helps in concentrating on the intrinsic powers of the heart, navel and chakras. The practitioner is supposed to close his eyes and mentally direct attention to the centre of the eyebrows.

■ **MADHYATRAATAK:** This involves gazing continuously at any object made of metal or stone, at *Aum* written on a piece of paper, a crystal, the bridge of one's nose, the centre of one's eyebrows or at any nearby object without blinking one's eyes .

■ **BAHYATRAATAK:** This means gazing continuously without blinking at some distant object like the moon, star or the rising sun.

One acquires expertise in **Shaambhavi Mudra** by performing the Traatak Kriya. This *kriya* cures diseases of the eyes, improves eyesight and reduces lethargy, giddiness and laziness. One also obtains the power of hypnotism from this *kriya*.

6. **Kapaalbhaati:** One's skull (including all the organs in the skull) is called **kapaal** and **bhaati**

is to illuminate, brighten or make brilliant. Kapaalbhaati is a process in which the organs in the skull, mainly the brain and the small brain, benefit tremendously. The process involves deep exhalation of the life force at considerable speed — just like the bellows of the ironsmith — to eliminate all ailments of the head and brain. In this process, air is inhaled automatically. *Gherand Samhita* describes three types of Kapaalbhaati — Vaatkram, Vyutkram and Sheetkarm.

- **VAATKRAM KAPAALBHAATI:** Sit straight and perform *rechak* from the left nostril by pressing the right nostril with the hand in the Pranayam posture. Then do *purak* (deep inhalation) from the left nostril quickly and then do rechak from the right nostril without performing *kumbhak* (holding the breath). Now, engage in *purak* from the right nostril and again *rechak* from the left nostril. Performing this *kriya* several times forcefully is called Vaatkram Kapaalbhaati. This *kriya* cures cough-related diseases.

- **VYUTKRAM KAPAALBHAATI:** The process of sniffing in lukewarm water from the nostrils and taking it out from the mouth is called Vyutkram Kapaalbhaati. This *kriya* removes cough-related diseases.

- **SHEETKARM KAPAALBHAATI:** Filling one's mouth with water by making a hissing sound and releasing it through the nostrils is called Sheetkarm Kapaalbhaati. This *kriya* improves the appearance of the practitioner, checks the process of ageing and cures cough-related diseases.

Therefore, Shatkarm, if performed as required, helps to flush out impurities and intoxicants from the body and regularises the body's metabolism. The Shatkarm of Hathyog transforms a man, makes him healthy, and increases his lifespan. It also rejuvenates him for Saadhna.

AASAN

The state in which the body achieves both stability and bliss is called **Aasan**. According to Sage Gherand:

Aasnaans samastaani yaavantoh Jeevjantavah
Chatursheetilakshaani shivena Kathithang pura
Teshaang madhye vishisthani Shodshonag shatkritan
Teshaang madhye martyaloke Dvaatringshadaasanang
shubham

(*Gherand Samhita*, 2/1-2)

This *sutra* implies that the number of aasans equals the number of living beings in this world. As there are supposed to be 84 lakh living beings, the number of aasans is regarded to be the same. *Gherand Samhita* has placed emphasis on 8,400 aasans and considered 84 of them to be superior and important. Of these, the following 32 aasans are considered especially beneficial to human beings and give us a sense of fulfilment: Siddhaasan, Padmaasan, Bhadraasan, Muktaasan, Vajrasan, Swastikaasan, Simhaasan, Gomukhaasan, Veeraasan, Dhanuraasan, Mritaasan, Guptaasan, Matsyaasan, Matsyendraasan, Gorakhaasan, Paschimottanaasan, Utkataasan,

Samkataasan, Mayuraasan, Kukkutaasan, Kurmaasan, Uttankurmaasan, Uttanmandukaasan, Vrikshaasan, Mandukaasan, Garudaasan, Vrishabhaasan, Shalabhaasan, Makaraasan, Ushtraasan, Bhujangaasan and Yogaasan. Hathyog Pradipika has identified **Siddhaasan, Padmaasan, Simhaasan** and **Bhadraasan** as the four most important aasans. Siddhaasan is considered to be the best from the point of Saadhna.

Kuryadattasanang sthairyymarogyam chaanglaaghvam
(Hathyog Pradipika, 1/17)

The above *sutra* says that regular practice of aasan makes the body calm, helps to lose fat and wards off diseases. The aasans that have been considered important are necessary for practising Pranayam and Dhyaan. A yoga practitioner can progress on the path of *saadhna* if he diligently performs even one aasan. That is why these aasans are called dhyaanaasan.

By practising these aasans regularly, one can become healthy and his ability to handle hunger, thirst, hatred and insult will improve. There is hardly any ailment in which aasans do not have a positive effect. In fact, yogaasan is a scientific way of preventing diseases. While practising yoga, focus your mind on the body and cultivate the belief that your health is improving rapidly. Then, let the aasans have their effect on your physical health. Otherwise, aasans may not show any result or benefit even if they are practised for years. If you are suffering from any disease, perform the aasan corresponding to it. But bear in mind that the practice of a wrong aasan may have an adverse effect and aggravate your problem.

MUDRA

Kriyas or actions that help attain perfection in pranayam and pratyaahaar are called **mudra**. The following 25 mudras have been described in *Gherand Samhita*: Mahamudra, Nabhomudra, Uddiyan Bandh, Jalandharbandh, Mulbandh, Mahabandh, Mahavedha, Khechari, Vipritkarani, Yoni, Vajroli, Shaktichalini, Taragi, Mandavi, Panchadharna (including five mudras), Ashwani, Paashani, Kaaki, Maatangi and Bhujangini.

Hathyog Pradipika mentions 10 such mudras: Mahaamudra, Mahaabandha, Mahaavedha, Khechari, Uddiyanbandh, Mulbandh, Jalandharbandh, Vipritkarani, Vajroli and Shaktichaalini.

Using these mudras during Hathyog ensures that the body's kundalini (cosmic energy) and chakras are awakened quickly. The nerve centre of energy also becomes active and results in proper circulation of energy throughout the body. Thus, you are cured of every disease.

PRATYAAHAAR

Our mind gets attracted to many things. The process of redirecting one's mind from these objects to one's *aatman* and keeping it under control is called **Pratyaahaar**. Pranayam is essential for Pratyaahaar as it controls the speed of life force and puts a brake on the fickle mind. In this way, the sense organs — which usually follow the mind — become serene and look inwards.

According to the *Vashishthha Samhita*, there are 18 sensitive spots in our body. These are toes, ankles, the middle of the thighs, underside of knees, knees, centre of the uterus, anal region, central body, genitals, navel, heart, base of the throat, palate, *nasamool* (root of the nostrils), central point between eyes, central point between eyebrows, head and *moordha* (base of the neck). Taking air from one of these points and placing them at some other point continuously is considered a good means of Pratyaahaar.

PRANAYAM

Stabilizing the flow of life force in our body's blood vessels is called **Pranayam**. It is made up of two words, pran and *ayam*. **Pran** is the energy or life force that resides in the body and keeps the body and the mind fit. It is the basis of all activities of the body and mind. Based on their location and work performed, pran is of five types (Panchpran): Pran, Apaan, Samaan, Vyaan and Udaan. Pranayama is a scientific method of controlling the breath, leading to better health for both mind and body.

Pran or the life force should be controlled in the same way as lions, elephants or tigers are tamed — gradually and with patience. Life force, when controlled under compulsion, has a negative impact. By doing Pranayam in a wrong way, you can suffer from hiccups, breathing ailments, cough, headache, pain in eyes, ears and fever.

Pranayam cleanses all the 72,000 blood vessels of our body. The power of pran cures all diseases of the body and mind. It helps you to slim down and radiate vigour. In the process, your mind is filled with happiness and your kundalini power within you is awakened. Just as fire purifies gold, Pranayam purifies and cures ailments of the sense organs. In yogic discipline, it is believed that an ailment occurs in an organ when the circulation of life force in that organ gets imbalanced and disorganized. Pranayam, therefore, ensures optimum circulation of life force in every part of the body and helps to eradicate diseases.

Hathyog Pradipika describes eight types of Pranayam:

Suryabhedanamujjayi sitkari shitli tatha
bhastrika brammari murchha plavinityasta kumbhakah
(*Hathyog Pradipika*, 2/44)

These are: Suryabhedan, Ujjaayi, Sitkaari, Shitli, Bhastrika, Bhraamari, Moorchha and Plaavini. According to Hathyog, before doing these Pranayams, the blood vessels of the body should be cleansed by performing **Naadishodhan Pranayam**. This Pranayam, which plays an important role in preventing and curing diseases, keeps a person healthy.

DHYAAN

This means contemplating the Almighty residing in your heart. During Dhyaan, the practitioner's mind becomes free from bondages, attains complete knowledge and focuses on the inner self. As the mind is empowered by Dhyaan, a practitioner attains peace, concentration, happiness and bliss. It also increases love and compassion for others. Dhyaan helps you to concentrate on your work without focusing on pride or the result of the work. This keeps you in a state of non-attachment.

SAMAADHI

Dhyaan turns into Samaadhi when it is practised for a long period. In the state of Samaadhi, a person loses awareness of the self, his mind becomes tranquil and ego and attachment disappear. The practitioner sees only the target and, like a seer, is confined to his innermost self. It is then that the kundalini power of a person is awakened, liberating him completely.

ADVANTAGES OF HATHYOG

Describing the advantages of the seven parts of Hathyog, *Gherand Samhita* says:

Shatkarmana shodhanam cha aasanen bhaveddhridham
Mudrayaa sthirata chaiva pratyaharen dhirataa
Pranayamallaaghavam cha dhyanatp ratykshamatmani
Samadhina nirliptam cha muktiravana samsayah
(*Gherand Samhita*, 1/10-11)

This means, the body is cleansed by Shatkarm, becomes firm and strong by Aasans, stable with the help of mudras and patient as a result of Pratyaahaar.

Pranayam makes the body feel lighter, Dhyaan results in self-realisation and one is liberated when Samaadhi results in a sense of detachment.

Thus, the practice of Hathyog prevents every disease of the body and mind. It gives rise to *yogaani*, which annihilates impurities of our body.

Vapuhakrishtvam vadane prasannata
naadassaputatvam nayane sunirmale,
Arogata bindujayoognidipanam
naadivishuddirhathasiddhilaxnam
(*Hathyog Pradipika*, 2/78)

This *sutra* means that the body of a Hathyog practitioner becomes slim, his face reflects his happiness, he becomes aware of the sound within (*naad*), his eyes become clear, all disorders of his body are eliminated, his blood vessels are cleansed and purified and he, thereby, attains good health.

Pran Oorja Yog

Pran or "life-force" is the basis of all our physical activities and movement. It keeps our entire body regulated and healthy. According to the philosophy of yoga, the body remains physically fit as long as the life-force is circulated properly in it. If there is any hindrance or irregularity in its flow, the body becomes ill.

Pran Oorja Yog is a scientific method of regulating energy in the body by removing diseases from their root. **Panchkosha**s are cleansed and stagnant faecal matter, foreign bodies, toxic elements, polluted substances and air are excreted. This yoga has a positive impact on all parts of the body, including the nerves and veins, tissues, endocrine glands, even little cells and, thereby, on all activities of the body. The flow of life-force is facilitated and the energy of the body is unified with the super energy scattered in the cosmos.

Pran Oorja Yog empowers and invigorates the sense organs and replaces negative thoughts with positive ones. Pran Oorja Yog can be easily practised at home. With regular practise, this yoga brings happiness and bliss and increases the power of the mind.

Pran Oorja Yog conforms to the definition of health given in Ayurveda. Describing the features of a healthy person, Maharshi Sushruta has said the following:

Samadhoshah samaagnishcha samadhaatu malakriyah
Prasannaatmendriya manaha swastha ityabhidiyate

A healthy person is one whose three *doshas* — **Vayu** (wind), **Pitta** (bile) and **Kapha** (cough) — *dhatus* (tissues) and *malas* (excretory functions) are in balance and his soul and body — *indriyas* (higher functions) and *mana* (mind) — are happy. This person will be healthy, in a disease-free state and really balanced.

With the passage of time, the human body becomes old, frail and weak. The process of ageing is often hastened by one's carelessness and faulty lifestyle. Pran Oorja Yog, however, can slow premature ageing and can help one appear youthful for a longer time.

Most people think or plan to do yoga when they fall ill, but this is an incorrect approach. Practise Pran Oorja Yog regularly and do not allow even a minor disease to attack your body.

Two things are vital for a healthy disposition. First, a healthy person should be protected from diseases and second, people suffering from diseases should be cured. By following a routine and using preventive measures, one can prevent diseases. Corporate life and modern lifestyle hardly ensure good health. In a relentless quest to earn more money, most modern-day executives work hard and do not pay much attention to food and health. In addition to reckless eating habits and lack of self-control, they have a gnawing fear of losing what they possess, and an insatiable desire to acquire what they don't have. More often than not, they are overcome by stress, anger, fear, confusion and arrogance. These things have a negative effect on their health. Attempts to replenish lost health with the wealth one has accumulated are often futile. A better alternative is to adopt the *madhya marg* (middle path) by paying attention to requirements of the body and practising Pran Oorja Yog even while working hard to earn money. In this way, a yoga practitioner can prevent lifestyle diseases and can remain happy and upbeat. A healthy body is like a crown whose true worth is understood only by a person who is seriously ill. It sure is a good idea to practise Pran Oorja Yog every day for at least half an hour.

PRAN OORJA YOG IS A 30-MINUTE PRACTICE

Keep aside at least 30 minutes each day for yourself, for your body. That is the duration of Pran Oorja Yog. The time span of each exercise has been indicated. If practised early in the morning, its affect remains for the whole day long and one feels light and fresh.

Pran Oorja Yog should be practised in its proper sequence, with the firm belief that one's body and mind are becoming healthy. In this manner, the practitioner will observe that this 30-minute practice is effective for the rest of the 23½ hours of the day. Following this, no further practice is required.

Today, people are keen to do yoga but don't know which aasan or Pranayam they should opt for. They aren't sure which aasan will be beneficial to them and cure their ailments. Pran Oorja Yog can be done in the comfort of one's home with little or no investment and will give quick and early results.

Pran Oorja Yog, which has been conceived and programmed after years of experience, has a solution to all your queries. Practise it regularly to make your body shapely, strong and flexible and render it free of ailments.

SEQUENCE OF PRAN OORJA YOG
Pran Oorja Yog is a modern and effective system of yoga. Based on the sequence described in the yog shastras, it is completely scientific. In this system, the body gets cleansed quickly, acquires flexibility, becomes light, firm and free of disease.

According to yog shastras, during the practice of yoga, the important *kriyas* of Shatkarm should be performed first. This cleanses the body internally. Thereafter, one should practise the aasans. The performance of Shatkarm before aasans ensures that faecal matter is discharged from the body. This increases benefits of the aasans. After this, the practice of Pranayam has been prescribed. You can reap the maximum benefit from Pranayam when you practise it in the proper sequence given. It is beneficial to do Dhyaan after Pranayam as it makes the mind serene and increases concentration. Thus, the practise of yoga graduates from the crude to the refined or subtle. The sequence of Pran Oorja Yog has been prepared keeping in view its scientific nature and shows astonishing results after a few prescribed exercises are performed.

The first exercise that has been described is **Kapaalbhaati**. This is a *kriya* of Shatkarm that cleanses the body with the help of air. After this, Agnisaar Kriya — which involves minor movements of legs and is included in Shatkarm — should be performed. Then, one has to do a selection of aasans that cure lifestyle diseases.

After the aasans, perform three Pranayams. The first among them is the **Anulom-Vilom Pranayam**. According to yog shastras, it can clean all 72,000 blood vessels of the body. This is also called **Naadishodhan Pranayam**. Naadishodhan ensures that other Pranayams do not have any side effect on the body.

Next is the **Bhastrika Pranayam** because Anulom-Vilom Pranayam results in a regular and balanced flow of air in the *swar* (nasal sound) of the nostrils — Chandra Swar on the left and Surya Swar on the right. According to yogic belief, disturbances in the *swar* lead to ailments, i.e. when one *swar* continues for a longer duration than normal, it causes a disease either in the mind or in the body. Anulom-Vilom Pranayam regulates these *swar*s by balancing the flow of life force in the body and mind. If a person starts practising Bhastrika Pranayam without regulating the *swar*s through Anulom-Vilom, the life force will flow only in that *swar* which is active at that time. This will result in an increase in the flow of life force in one *swar* compared to the other and disturb the balance. This, in turn, may have a harmful effect on the body.

Bhramari Pranayam should be done after Bhastrika Pranayam. Pran Oorja Yog ends with the **Dhyaanatmak Shavaasan**.

Preparing for Pran Oorja Yog
1. Practise Pran Oorja Yog in the morning on an empty stomach after your daily ablutions. Wear loose clothes and sit on the ground, in an airy space, by spreading a mat or a blanket.
2. During summer, it is better to do Pran Oorja Yog on the terrace, verandah or lawn.

3. The place where yoga is practised should be clean and free from houseflies, mosquitoes, dust, smoke and foul odour.
4. The mat should be spread on an even surface.
5. If you intend practising in the evening, you should relieve yourself 4-5 hours after lunch.
6. Women should not practise Pran Oorja Yog while menstruating or during pregnancy. However, during pregnancy, women can do those aasans that ensure better nutrition to the foetus, improve the mother's health, and increase chances of normal delivery. After 2-3 months of normal delivery, one can practise this sequence.
7. Face the North or East direction while practising yoga and keep your *guru* in mind.

Points to remember

1. Keep your mind calm and happy and refrain from anger, irritation or hurry.
2. Do not let tension appear on the nerves, nose, ears, neck and eyes during the exercise. Keep only the body active and inhale and exhale through the nose.
3. Take into consideration your age, physical and mental condition, flexibility, capacity, environment and time.
4. If you feel an urge to relieve yourself during the exercise, stop and resume the exercise later.
5. Do not practise Pran Oorja Yog when you have fever, severe cough and cold.
6. Do not practise this yoga in haste and avoid force and jolts of any kind. Do each exercise slowly, with full conviction and concentrate on your body and breath.

7. Practise yoga with your eyes closed and focus on your body. Be firm in your conviction that this yoga will eliminate all diseases from your body and keep you fit. Continue to believe that you are becoming healthier because it is our thinking that aggravates or cures diseases.

Steps to follow after doing Pran Oorja Yog

1. After the exercise, sit silently and peacefully with your eyes closed. Think about God and your *guru*.
2. Fold the mat that you had spread on the floor for the exercise and keep it in a secure place. Do not use it for any other purpose.
3. Take a bath after half an hour. You can drink water after 15-20 minutes but only after you have kept it in your mouth for some time. You may eat after half an hour.
4. Avoid speaking loudly and losing your temper after the exercise. As far as possible, keep your mind calm and blissful.
5. If the schedule and place are fixed, the exercise becomes more beneficial. Continue practising yoga even when you are away from home.
6. If needed, this exercise can be done twice a day. Start Pran Oorja Yog by chanting *Aum*. Face either the East or the North and sit in the meditative posture. Keep the back and neck straight in line and close your eyes.

Then keep your hands in the Gyan Mudra posture and smile while you concentrate on your breath. Take a deep breath and exhale the air while chanting *Aum*. Chant *Aum* thrice. Remain seated and concentrate on your breathing again. Start Kapaalbhaati kriya.

SCHEDULE OF PRAN OORJA YOG

Yogic Exercise	Time
Kapaalbhaati	5 minutes
Micro exercises of the legs	1 minute
Agnisaar Kriya	1 minute
Taadaasan	1 minute
Micro exercises of the hands	1 minute
Urdhvahastottanaasan	1 minute
Uttaanpaadaasan	1 minute
Katichakraasan	1 minute
Pavanmuktaasan	1 minute
Bhujangaasan	1 minute
Naukaasan	1 minute
Mandookaasan	1 minute
Anulom-vilom Pranayam	5 minutes
Micro exercises of the neck	1 minute
Bhastrikaa Pranayam	5 minutes
Bhraamari Pranayam	1 minute
Shavaasan	2 minutes
Total time	**30 minutes**

CHANTING AUM

Start **Pran Oorja Yog** by chanting *Aum*. Face either the East or the North and sit in the meditative posture. Keep the back and neck straight in a line and close your eyes. Then keep your hands in the Gyan Mudra posture *(see p. 93)* and smile while you concentrate on your breath. Take a deep breath and exhale the air while chanting *Aum*. Chant *Aum* thrice. Remain seated and concentrate on your breathing again. Start Kapaalbhaati Kriya.

KAPAALBHAATI

The process of exhaling with immense speed again and again is called **Kapaalbhaati**. It is made up of two words — *kapaal* and *bhaati*. Kapaal means head and Bhaati means to brighten or understand the head. Thus, Kapaalbhaati helps to activate or rejuvenate energy centres in the head by cleansing the brain and increasing cognitive and perceptive vision.

Procedure: Sit in any of the aasans like Padmaasan, Swastikaasan, Siddhaasan or Sukhaasan and keep your back in a straight line. Your chest should bulge out. Place your hands on your knees, as in Gyan Mudra *(see p. 93)*, close your eyes and sit comfortably. Then concentrate on your breath and its rhythm, without keeping your stomach slack or loose. To perform Kapaalbhaati, push your stomach inside , below the navel, with a jerk, and squeeze the muscles of the stomach. Simultaneously, exhale forcefully through the nose, making a hissing sound. After that, relax the stomach muscles — which you had squeezed — and inhale air without making any sound. Refrain from exerting any pressure while inhaling and allow air to go inside your body naturally. Push your stomach inside again with a jerk and exhale the air noisily. This practice should be done continuously. Exhale quickly as many times as possible and when you feel exhausted, sit quietly till your breathing resumes its normal pace.

Duration: Initially, breathe 20-30 times or as much as possible in one round. As your practice increases, the speed and number of breaths will also increase.

Subsequently, you can practise for two to three minutes at the rate of 40-60 breaths. Do 2-3 rounds of Kapaalbhaati.

Your heartbeat and blood pressure will increase slightly during Kapaalbhaati but will normalize later.

Precautions: While performing Kapaalbhaati, do not make any sound from your throat. This can dry up your mouth and cause irritation. Your voice too can become hoarse. While exercising, only a hissing sound should come from your nostrils.

While doing Kapaalbhaati, your back and neck should be in a straight line and your chest should be bulging forward. Don't move any other part of your body except your stomach. Keep your face calm and peaceful and your eyes closed.

People suffering from cardiac diseases, high blood pressure and chronic asthma should not perform this exercise. But it can be practised at a slower pace if the disease is in control. This exercise is also prohibited for patients of hernia. In case of back pain, Kapaalbhaati may be practiced in the **Vajraasan** posture. If one is unable to sit on the ground, this exercise can be done while seated on a chair.

Resolution: While practising Kapaalbhaati, you should feel that with every breath you exhale, various ailments from your body are being expelled and your body is becoming free of diseases.

Centre of Dhyaan: Manipura Chakra

Advantages: Kapaalbhaati is a cleansing process that plays an important role in removing faecal matter, foreign objects and polluted air from inside the body with the help of air. With the purification of the body, the mind becomes relaxed.

In Kapaalbhaati, blood from your hands and legs starts flowing towards the stomach muscles and other parts, making the food pipe, stomach, small intestine, large intestine, gall bladder, pancreas, rectum, liver, kidney, testes and prostrate (in males), and the uterus and ovary (in females) healthier. It aids in curing ailments related to these organs.

Kapaalbhaati keeps thyroid and parathyroid glands, thymus gland, lungs and trachea well toned. An increase in the oxygen content of the blood results in the supply of this vital element to all cells and tissues. Kapaalbhaati also makes the heart muscles strong and supple and prevents cardiac diseases.

This exercise cures disorders like constipation, gas, diabetes, loss of appetite, indigestion and obesity. By regulating the secretion of digestive juices, it improves the digestive power. It helps in disorders of the prostrate gland and urinary tract. Kapaalbhaati is also helpful in curing female disorders like irregular menstruation, vaginal discharge and excessive bleeding. It helps remove tumours or glands and cures cough, cold and asthma. It is useful in treating skin diseases and preventing hair loss, hair breakage and premature greying. Kapaalbhaati can keep you feeling fresh throughout the day, cure every disease and improve your level of concentration.

MICRO EXERCISES OF THE LEGS

After practising Kapaalbhaati, spread both your legs in front and practise the following *kriya*:

Procedure: With both legs in front, place your hands behind you, on the ground. Then stretch both toes to the front and remain in that position for a while. After that, pull your feet backward by stretching and remain in that position for some time. Practise this 4-5 times daily.

Next, join your feet and try to move them together by rotating them from left to right, making a large circle. Then change the direction of the movement. While rotating the toes, the little toe should touch the ground. Perform this exercise 4-5 times. Now, relax your legs.

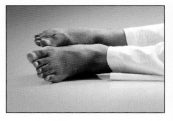 

Raise both knees, one by one, above the ground and put them on the surface with a jolt. Heels should keep touching the ground. Practise it 6-8 times.

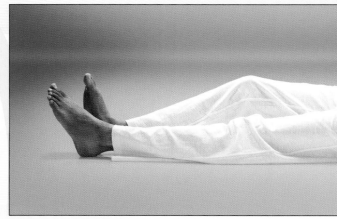

After this, you must do the **Titli Aasan**. Two exercises make up Titli Aasan. Fold your legs and bring them together so that the knees and the soles of both feet touch each other. Then hold the knees with your hands and raise them so that they touch each other. Put them back on the floor and repeat this action 3-4 times.

After that, hold your feet together with both hands and move your knees up and down quickly, like the wings of a butterfly. Practise this action 8-10 times.

Pace of Breathing: Take deep breaths during each exercise.

Resolution: During this exercise, concentrate only on your legs and imagine that they are becoming lighter and stronger.

Advantages: This exercise provides relief when your legs ache or feel numb, when you have pain in the heels and knees, swelling, muscle cramps, sciatica and varicose veins. It makes the legs sturdy and supple. Titli Aasan makes the thigh muscles and hip bones supple. It removes fatigue from your legs and makes you feel as light as a butterfly. This exercise also corrects urinary disorders.

AGNISAAR KRIYA

Agnisaar Kriya is also a part of Shatkarm. It can prevent and cure all stomach-related diseases. It is known as Agnisaar because it kindles and excites 13 types of *agni*s in the body (seven *dhatvagni*, five *bhootagni* and one *jatharagni*). It is also called **Bahnisaar** in the *Yog Shastra*.

Procedure: Stand erect with your feet a foot apart. Lean forward and place your hands on the thighs above the knees and loosen the stomach muscles. Now, inhale as much air as you can, then exhale it completely and push the lower portion of the stomach inside. Try to make the navel touch your

spinal chord. After that, release the stomach again and push it inside once more. Repeat this process several times and continue till you are able to hold your breath easily. After doing this exercise according to your capacity, bring the stomach back to its normal position and stand up, inhaling normally.

Duration: Agnisaar Kriya involves exhaling air from the body so continue to pump the stomach till you can hold your breath comfortably. Initially, the stomach will move only 8-10 times. After some practice, you may be able to move your stomach 20-30 times. Repeat this process 2-3 times.

Speed of breath: As Agnisaar Kriya entails exhaling air, do not inhale in the midst of the *kriya*. Stop the exercise if you feel out of breath and start the process again when your breathing becomes normal.

Precautions: This exercise should be done at a normal pace and with ease, without forcefully stopping your breathing. Move your stomach for as long as you feel comfortable. Those suffering from acidity, ulcer, hernia, colitis and slipped disc are advised not to do this exercise. Patients who have undergone stomach surgery or those who have

cardiac problems or hypertension should also avoid this exercise.

Resolution: While performing this *kriya*, one should concentrate on the stomach. Bear in mind that due to the movement of the stomach, the supply of blood towards it increases and all stomach-related ailments eventually get cured.

Centre of Dhyaan: Manipura Chakra

Advantages: Agnisaar Kriya puts pressure on the stomach that, in turn, has a positive impact on other parts of the body. Pumping the stomach during this *kriya* directly benefits the stomach, small intestine, large intestine, liver, pancreas, gall bladder, kidney, adrenal gland, uterus and ovary (in females) and prostrate gland (in males). It does so by increasing blood circulation. It has a positive effect on Samaan Vaayu and Apaan Vaayu (gas) that are situated under the heart. This *kriya* rejuvenates you by kindling 13 types of *agni*s in the body.

By eliminating foreign elements present in the body, Agnisaar Kriya cures constipation, gas, loss of appetite, weakness of intestine, urinary disorder and indigestion. It is especially recommended for those who suffer from poor health despite eating nutritious food.

A regular practice of Agnisaar Kriya helps in addressing ailments like diabetes and obesity. This exercise triggers the formation of insulin in the pancreas and also reduces extra flab on the stomach.

Agnisaar is believed to slow down the ageing process, thereby ensuring that one retains one's youth longer. It increases the body's energy and strength and rejuvenates it. By keeping stomach diseases at bay, this *kriya* helps to keep the practitioner fit.

TAADAASAN

Taad is the name of a tall and straight tree. **Taadaasan** is a posture that involves shaping the body like a *taad* (palm) tree.

Procedure: Stand erect after Agnisaar Kriya with your feet joined together. Bring both hands in front of your chest and interlock your fingers. After that, turn your joined palms in a way that the palm faces outwards and stretch. Now, raise your hands towards the sky while inhaling. Next, bring your hands slightly to the back of your head, keeping your elbows straight. Balance your body on your toes and raise the soles of your feet from the ground. Stretch your body upwards as much as possible. Breathe normally and stay in this position for some time. Return to the normal position by exhaling slowly and unlocking the palms. Bring your hands to their normal position or against the sides of your body.

Duration: Return to the normal position by staying in Taadaasan posture for 20-30 seconds. Do this aasan twice.

Pace of Breathing: Inhale air before getting into the aasan posture. Remain in the last stage of the aasan by taking a deep breath. Exhale as you return to the original position.

Precautions: Retain a happy facial expression while performing the aasan. Stretch only the body and not the face.

Resolution: While doing Taadaasan, concentrate on your body, first from toe to head, and then vice versa. Tell yourself that every muscle in your body and the joint of each bone is getting stretched and is becoming stronger and supple.

Centre of Dhyaan: Spinal Cord

Advantages: As an effect of the gravitational pull, our bodies gets pulled down all the time. In Taadaasan, the body is stretched upwards, as a result of which every muscle is toned. Taadaasan also strengthens the joints and bones and makes them strong and supple. The vertebra and back muscles get toned even as you stretch your backbone. This provides relief in back pain, slipped disc, neck pain, stiffness in the shoulder, arthritis and joint pain.

Taadaasan has a positive effect on the digestive system, respiratory system, skeletal system, nervous system and muscular system, and prevents diseases relating to them. This aasan helps in the treatment of asthma, breathing problems and cough and makes the chest and heart muscles supple. Laziness, fatigue, heaviness and stiffness can be kept at bay by practising this aasan. To energize yourself, you can do Taadaasan at any time of the day when you feel exhausted.

This aasan is recommended for increasing the height of children. The weight and pressure of the entire body falls on the lower part of the toe which, according to acupressure, controls sensitive points of the brain, sinus, eyes, nose, neck, pituitary gland, pineal gland, thyroid gland, parathyroid and thymus gland. By doing this aasan, you can keep these organs fit.

MICRO EXERCISES OF THE HANDS

Procedure: After Taadaasan, spread your legs apart. Keeping your hands on your shoulders, join both elbows in front, gradually raise them upwards and bring them to the back of your body. Now, bring the elbows to the front, and let them touch each other. Rotate the elbows in the opposite direction about 4-6 times.

In another exercise, hold the fingers of both hands together. Take your hands to the back of the head and stretch the left elbow towards the lower left side as much as possible. Repeat the same action with the right elbow. After doing this exercise 2-3 times, move your hands to the back of your head so that they can vigorously pull each other. Then gradually raise your head towards the sky. Practise this 2-3 times.

Duration: This exercise can be practised at any time of the day. Do the first exercise 4-6 times on the left side, and 4-6 times on the right side. Thereafter, do the second exercise 2-3 times.

Pace of Breathing: In the first exercise, raise the elbows while inhaling and lower your elbows while exhaling. In the second exercise, bring your hands down while inhaling and raise your hands while breathing out.

Resolution: While doing this exercise, have implicit faith that your hands, shoulder muscles, neck and joints are getting strengthened and becoming supple.

Advantages: This exercise eliminates stiffness in the shoulder, neck, back and joints and makes them flexible and supple, preventing cervical spondylitis.

URDHVAHASTOTTANAASAN

In this exercise, stretch both your hands upwards and bend your waist sideways. **Urdhvahastottanaasan** keeps the digestive system fit and helps remove flab from the body.

Procedure: After the micro exercises of the hands, stand straight and spread your legs 1 to 1.5ft apart. Now, interlock fingers of your hand as in Taadaasan, reverse the joined palms and stretch your hands upwards. Then bend your waist towards the left while exhaling and stay in that position for as long as possible. Keep your elbows straight, head upwards, knees straight and the soles of your feet firmly placed on the ground. Breathe normally, keeping your eyes closed. To return to the normal position, keep your waist straight and inhale. Repeat the action on the right side.

Duration: Practise this exercise twice on the right-hand side and twice on the left. Obese people may do this exercise 8-10 times.

Pace of Breathing: Exhale air while bending your waist and inhale while returning to the original position. In the aasan position, breathe normally.

Precautions: Don't do the aasan in haste and avoid jolts while attaining the posture and returning back to the original position. Bend your waist as much as possible without exerting unnecessary force. In the event of back pain, don't do this aasan.

Resolution: In the last stage of the aasan, close your eyes and keep your face peaceful and happy. Firmly believe that this stretching posture will make your waist flexible and improve its shape.

Advantages: Every organ of the stomach is massaged by this aasan. It improves the digestive system, makes the intestine active and cures constipation and gas. By addressing obesity-related problems, this aasan improves your looks and makes you strong. With regular practise, the extra flab disappears and the waist becomes slim. By regulating the secretion of insulin and activating the pancreas, this aasan prevents and cures diabetes. It is also effective in treating defects relating to the backbone, aches in the back and waist, neck pain and stiff neck. As a result of this exercise, muscles of the hands, legs, thighs, back, waist and neck become supple and strong.

UTTAANPADAASAN

Uttaanpada is made up of two words — *uttaan* and *pada*. *Uttaan* means to raise something upwards, and *pada* means leg. Therefore, the aasan in which legs are raised upwards is called **Uttaanpadaasan**.

Procedure: Lie comfortably on your back in Shavaasan after Urdhvahastottanaasan. Concentrate on your breathing for some time. Then put the palms of your hands on the ground near your thighs. Join your legs, including the soles and toes, and stretch the toes towards the front. Inhale and raise both legs together, pushing the floor with your hands. Stop moving the legs when they make an angle of 60 degrees from the ground and breathe normally. Remain in this position for as long as you can and bring the legs back to the ground, first making 45 degrees and then 30 degrees. Rest in Shavaasan for a while.

Duration: Practise this aasan twice during the day. To ward off obesity, keep moving the legs up and down, without resting them on the ground.

Pace of Breathing: Inhale while raising the legs and breathe normally while in the aasan position. Return to the normal position, exhaling.

Precautions: Patients of slipped disc, backache, high blood pressure, hernia and cardiac diseases may perform this aasan by raising one leg. Do not stretch your face while doing this aasan, and remain in the aasan position for as long as you can without exerting any force.

Resolution: Close your eyes in the last stage of the aasan and ensure that your face radiates happiness. While experiencing the effects of the aasan on the body, imagine that your digestive system, respiratory system, heart and brain are becoming healthier.

Centre of Dhyaan: Manipura Chakra

Advantages: In this aasan, the legs are raised above other parts of the body. This improves the blood circulation from the legs to the stomach, chest and face. Raising the legs also puts pressure on the stomach, thereby strengthening its muscles, removing extra flab and tightening slack muscles. With the strengthening of the stomach and lower abdomen, the digestive system becomes strong and hernia can be prevented. You can also cure inflammation of the navel, constipation, gas and loss of appetite. The pancreas is activated to produce insulin that helps in the prevention of diabetes. This aasan also benefits the heart and lungs and prevents cough and cold. The blood pressure remains under control and even disorders related to hair are addressed.

KATICHAKRAASAN

Procedure: Practise **Katichakraasan** after doing Uttaanpaadaasan. Put both hands under your head with the elbows on the ground. Fold the left leg at the knee and place the sole of the foot on the right thigh While exhaling, try to take the left-bent knee to the right side by bending from the waist and let it touch the floor. Turn the neck towards the left. Now, close your eyes and breathe normally. Remain in this posture for as much time as you can and then bring the knee back to the normal position and straighten the leg. Repeat this exercise by folding the right knee.

Duration: Practise Katichakraasan twice, using each leg separately. Return to the original position after remaining in this aasan for a while.

Pace of Breathing: Exhale while moving the knee towards the floor. Breathe normally in the last stage

of this exercise. When returning to the original posture, lift the leg while inhaling and return the leg to its previous position, while exhaling.

Precautions: Be careful to guard against any jolt while doing this aasan. Don't do it in haste or by force. Keep the legs close to the ground as much as possible.

Resolution: Close your eyes and concentrate on your backbone, waist, hips and thighs where the aasan is expected to have the most effect. Imagine that the flexibility of these organs is increasing and energy in your body is getting balanced.

Advantages: Any stiffness in the body disturbs the balance of energy flow. Katichakraasan corrects the stiffness of the backbone, thighs and hips and makes the body flexible. It also regulates the flow of energy in the body.

By strengthening the stomach muscles and removing extra flab from the waist, this aasan makes you look slim and attractive. Kidneys, liver, intestines, pancreas, rectum and bladder become healthy due to pressure and tightness exerted while doing this exercise. By doing this aasan, you can also get relief from back pain, sciatica, constipation, gas, diabetes and obesity.

PAWANMUKTAASAN

True to its name, **Pawanmuktaasan** ejects polluted air and gas from inside the body and gives us relief.

Procedure: Practise Pawanmuktaasan after Katichakraasan. Lie straight on your back and fold both your legs at the knees. Then raise the legs, bring the knees towards the chest and hold the legs tight with the hands. Exhale and using your hands, push the legs towards the stomach. Now, raise the head and place your chin between the knees. Breathe normally, close your eyes, and remain in this position for some time. You can swing to and fro on your back and can also roll over to your right and left.

While returning to the normal position, first, bring down your head. Next, open the hands and bring them down along with the legs, inhaling air. Lie down in Shavaasan.

Duration: Practise this exercise twice. Remain in this posture for as much time as possible. Don't go back to the normal posture at once with a jolt as that will not give you the full benefits of this aasan.

Pace of Breathing: Raise the legs while inhaling and press the legs onto the stomach while exhaling. Breathe normally during the aasan after you have attained the posture. Inhale while returning to the normal position.

Precautions: If you are suffering from pain in the legs, do not attempt to hold the legs from above. Instead, hold your thighs. In case of pain in the neck

or hip, refrain from raising the head and swinging back and forth. Do the aasan while keeping the head on the ground.

Resolution: Close your eyes during the aasan and concentrate on the stomach, which is affected directly by this aasan. Think that the pressure that is being exerted on the stomach will tighten it and make the digestive system healthy.

Centre of Dhyaan: Manipura Chakra

Advantages: In this exercise, the thighs put pressure directly on the stomach, as a result of which, Apaan Vaayu situated in the large intestine gets expelled from the body. The pressure thus exerted helps to prevent and cure constipation, gas, acidity and loss of appetite. This exercise increases blood circulation to the heart and lungs and helps to control diseases like asthma, breathlessness, cough and cold.

When one returns to the normal position after this aasan, the blood that had rushed towards the chest starts returning to other organs and strengthens the stomach, liver, pancreas, small intestine, large intestine, bladder and kidney. It removes impurities accumulated in these organs. This exercise helps women, and other patients of hernia and back pain.

BHUJANGAASAN

This involves raising the upper half of the body in such a way that it resembles a *bhujang* (snake) raising its hood. Hence, the name **Bhujangaasan** or aasan of a snake.

Procedure: Lie on your stomach after doing Pawanmuktaasan. Place your forehead on the ground and join the toes and soles of both feet. Place your palms on the ground near your chest, keep your elbows elevated and the body relaxed.

Now, inhale and raise your head upwards along with the chest and shoulders, keeping the pressure on your hands. Bend the waist gradually towards the back, the neck backwards and raise the upper half of your body right up to the navel. All this while, keep your legs joined and breathe normally. In this posture, bend the neck to the left and look at your feet. Repeat the process by bending towards the right side. After that, slowly return to the original position while inhaling. Relax in the Makaraasan position by keeping your forehead on the floor, your palms under the head on the floor and your legs opened.

Duration: Repeat this aasan twice. Stay in the position of the aasan for as long as possible.

Pace of Breathing: Breathe in while raising the upper portion of your body in Bhujangaasan. Resume normal breathing once you have attained the correct posture. After that, return to the original position, exhaling.

Precautions: Don't bend your waist in haste or force yourself while doing this aasan. Bend your waist gradually, without hurting yourself. Avoid practising Bhujangaasan if you are suffering either from hernia or from peptic ulcer.

Resolution: Close your eyes while doing the aasan and concentrate on the waist, neck, stomach and chest, one after the other, imagining that they are becoming healthy, flexible and strong.

Centre of Dhyaan: Vishudhhi Chakra.

Advantages: While doing our daily chores, we usually keep the neck and hip region bent forwards. This causes pain in these parts. The backward bend in Bhujangaasan gives flexibility to the backbone and strengthens the hip and neck muscles. This aasan is effective in preventing back pain, slipped disc, sciatica and cervical spondylitis.

Bhujangaasan strengthens the ovary and uterus and helps prevent gynaecological problems like irregular and painful menstruation and leucorrhoea.

People afflicted with constipation, indigestion and loss of appetite will also benefit from Bhujangaasan. The exercise also increases the capacity of lungs, tones the entire nervous system, and has a positive impact on the thyroid, parathyroid, thymus and adrenal glands.

NAUKAASAN

As the name itself suggests, **Naukaasan** involves emulating the shape of a *nauka* (boat).

Procedure: Do Naukaasan after Bhujangaasan. Lie on your stomach and spread both hands towards the head, keeping both legs joined. Join your palms together and do a *namaste*, making the forehead touch the ground. Then stretch the hands and legs towards the front and back, respectively, inhaling air. Raise your hands, head and chest from the front and the feet, knees and thighs from the lower end, allowing only the stomach to touch the ground. Stretch the hands and feet as much as you can and breathe in and out normally. After that, gradually return to the normal position and rest for a while in Makaraasan posture by placing both palms under the head and spreading the legs apart.

Duration: Try to stay in this aasan for as long as possible and repeat this exercise twice.

Pace of Breathing: Inhale deeply while assuming the posture. Breathe normally after attaining the posture and return to the original position, exhaling.

Precautions: You should not practise this aasan in haste or with a jerk. Those who suffer from backache,

slipped disc, osteoporosis, heart ailments and high blood pressure can do this aasan by raising one hand and one leg. Those suffering from hernia, peptic ulcer, wounds in the intestine and those who have undergone stomach surgery should not practise this aasan.

Resolution: In the last stage of the aasan, close your eyes and concentrate on your body. Think with conviction that your muscular system, waist muscles, hands and legs are becoming stronger.

Centre of Dhyaan: Manipura Chakra or Vishudhhi Chakra.

Advantages: By doing these exercises, muscles of the waist, shoulders, thighs and hips become strong and flexible, reducing backaches and preventing hernia. The nervous system also improves. This aasan puts the complete weight of your body on the stomach and strengthens the stomach muscles, intestine, liver, abdomen, pancreas and kidney, increases the appetite and improves blood circulation.

MANDUKAASAN

In **Mandukaasan**, the body acquires the shape of a frog (*manduk* in Sanskrit). This aasan exerts pressure on kidneys and makes them function better and remedies urinary disorders.

Procedure: After doing Naukaasan, sit in Vajraasan posture by folding the knees. Now, press the thumb under the other four fingers and close the palms to make fists.

Place both fists on either side of the navel, with the inner side of the fist touching the stomach. Inhale, exhale and then push the stomach inside. Bend from the waist so that the chest is close to the knees. The elbows should be protruding on either side of the body. Close your eyes, raise your head and try to remain in this posture for a while, breathing normally. Inhale and return to the original position. Open your fists, come back to the Vajraasan posture, and then spread your legs outwards.

Duration: Mandukaasan should be practised twice a day. Patients of diabetes may do this exercise 6-8 times. Although it is beneficial to stay in Mandukaasan for as long as possible, do not increase the duration forcibly.

Pace of Breathing: In this aasan, all the air has to be breathed out of the body. Therefore, sufficient air should be inhaled before the aasan. Exhale while you are bending the body forward and breathe normally once you are in the aasan posture. Exhale while returning to the original position.

Precautions: Do not bend the body forward if you suffer from slipped disc, osteoporosis and back pain. In such cases, sit in Vajraasan and keep your stomach pressed with your fists. If your knee is aching, do not sit in Vajraasan. Instead, do the aasan by sitting on a chair and dangling your legs.

Resolution: During the last stage of the aasan, close your eyes and concentrate on the pressure that is being exerted on the stomach. Think with conviction that your entire digestive system is getting toned up and that your obesity is decreasing.

Centre of Dhyaan: Manipura Chakra.

Advantages: Mandukaasan tones the stomach muscles and is beneficial for the stomach, small intestine, large intestine, gall bladder, pancreas, rectum, liver, reproductive organs and kidneys. Do this aasan to eliminate diseases like constipation, gas, loss of appetite and indigestion.

Mandukaasan also helps diabetes patients by making the pancreas active and triggering the production of insulin in the body. Practise this aasan to regulate the functioning of your adrenal gland and to cure urinary disorders. Patients of hernia can benefit from this aasan. Mandukaasan also strengthens the lungs and heart, which ultimately helps to cure asthma.

ANULOM-VILOM PRANAYAM

Pranayam should be practised after doing various exercises. The first pranayam to be practised is Anulom-Vilom Pranayam. **Anulom-Vilom Pranayam** is also called **Naadishodhan Pranayam**. According to the *Yog Shastra*, Pranayam should begin with Anulom-Vilom because it cleanses all the 72,000 blood vessels of the body and makes the three main naadis — Idaa, Pingla and Sushumna — supple.

Procedure: Sit in a meditative posture. Keep your back and neck in a straight line and close your eyes. Now, bring your right hand in the pranayam posture and keep it on the nostrils. To get into the pranayam mudra, keep the index and middle fingers straight and close the right nostril with the thumb. With the index and middle fingers in the middle of the forehead, i.e. at the Ajnana Chakra, exhale air gradually through the left nostril. Now, breathe in through the left nostril. After inhaling as much air as you can, close the left nostril with your ring finger and small finger, remove your thumb from the right nostril and exhale

the air gradually out of the body through it. Then inhale through the right nostril. Next, put the thumb on the right nostril and breathe out from the left nostril by removing the fingers from it. This completes one cycle of Anulom-Vilom Pranayam.

Duration: Complete at least 11 cycles of this pranayam.

Pace of Breathing: While doing this exercise, no breathing sound should be audible. The speed of inhalation and exhalation should be so slow that even a small wad of cotton put near the nostrils should not move. Ensure that the time taken during rechak is double the time taken during purak.

Precautions: Those suffering from back ache and pain in the knee should practise pranayam sitting on a chair.

Resolution: Close your eyes during pranayam.

Imagine that Sushumna Naadi is being awakened by friction of Idaa and Pingla Naadis and that energy is flowing right from Muladhar Chakra to Sahasraar Chakra. Believe that your entire body is being cleansed and made healthy.

Centre of Dhyaan: Aajya Chakra.

Advantages: All blood vessels and veins are cleansed by the practice of Anulom-Vilom Pranayam. The energy in the body gets organized and starts flowing upwards. It cures diseases of the muscular system and is beneficial in arthritis, flatulence, varicose veins, acidity and sinusitis. Your thinking becomes positive and you learn to overcome tension, anger, worry, fretfulness, anxiety, uneasiness, high blood pressure, migraine and lack of sleep. With the regular practice of Anulom-Vilom Pranayam, your power of concentration, patience, resoluteness, decision-making ability and creativity will soon increase.

MICRO EXERCISES FOR THE NECK

Procedure:
1. After Anulom-Vilom Pranayam, sit and spread your legs out in front. Place your hands on the floor behind. Slowly move your neck backwards and gradually return to the original position.
2. Bring your neck to the left side as much as possible. Take it back to the original position and then bring it to the right side.
3. Bend your neck to the left so that it touches the shoulder. Do the same on the right side.
4. Keeping the back of the neck loose, rotate it in a semi-circle.
5. Fold your legs and sit. Interlock fingers of your hands and take them to the back of your head. Inhale and push your hands simultaneously towards the front and your head towards your back. Similarly, apply opposite pressure on the head with the help of your hands. Put the right palm on the right side of the head (near the right ear), apply opposite pressure. Repeat this on the left hand side.

Duration: Practise each exercise 2-3 times.

Pace of Breathing: Do deep breathing in every exercise.

70

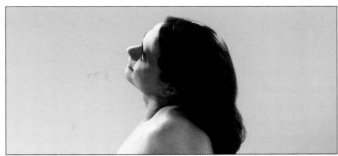

Resolution: Believe that your neck muscles are becoming stronger and flexible.

Centre of Dhyaan: Vishuddhi Chakra.

Advantages: In addition to strengthening the neck, these exercises address aches in the neck, stiff neck, twisting of the neck, swelling, numbness, cervical spondylitis etc. Practising these exercises prevents the occurrence of these disorders.

BHASTRIKA PRANAYAM

Practise **Bhastrika Pranayam** after doing micro exercises of the neck. Sit in any meditative posture, with your back and neck in a straight line. Place your hands on the knees as in Gyan Mudra and close your eyes. Now concentrate on inhalation and exhalation. Exhale to the maximum capacity through both nostrils then inhale through both nostrils as much air as you can. Exhale all the air again, without holding your breath. Continue to inhale and exhale heavily for a while. After doing the exercise to your capacity, breathe out all the air at one go. Then, start normal breathing and sit in the meditative posture.

Duration: Bhastrika Pranayam should be practised 30-40 times in a cycle or according to one's capacity. Do two or three cycles of this pranayam.

Pace of Breathing: In this exercise, many normal breaths are combined to form a single deep and long breath. You should inhale and exhale to your capacity, but keep the speed moderate.

Precautions: When you breathe in, your lungs should expand — not your stomach. Be happy and don't move your body while practising Bhastrika Pranayam. If you suffer from high blood pressure, migraine or cardiac disorders, inhale and exhale normally.

Resolution: Close your eyes and think that the air that you are inhaling is toning up your five prans — Pran, Apaan, Samaan, Vyaan and Udaan. You must believe that the Panchkosh is being purified, the energy centre is awakening and the cosmic power flowing inside you is uniting you with the supreme power. Think that the exhalation is purifying your body and mind and making you feel lighter.

Centre of Dhyaan: Sushumna Naadi.

Advantages: This exercise corrects and balances the three doshas of Vaat, Pitta and Kapha. According to Ayurveda, about 140 kinds of diseases may be caused due to an imbalance of the three doshas. During this exercise, more pure air goes inside the body and more impure air or carbon dioxide is exhaled out. This pranayam rejuvenates all cells, tissues, tendons, arteries and veins in the body and makes you feel fresh and energetic. Practise this pranayam to keep your digestive system, heart, lungs, brain and endocrine glands healthy, and to treat loss of appetite, indigestion, constipation, asthma, impurities in blood and certain skin diseases. By doing this exercise, your mental tension subsides and you acquire peace of mind. This also helps a person attain spirituality by awakening the Chakras and the power of Kundalini.

BHRAAMARI PRANAYAM

Procedure: After Bhastrika Pranayam, practise **Bhraamari Pranayam**. Sit in any meditative posture, keep your back and neck straight, and close your eyes. First, exhale the air slowly. Then, inhale as much air as possible. Now exhale, making a humming sound like that of a bee. Close both your ears with your thumbs to remain undisturbed by external noise. Keep the two index fingers on the forehead and close both eyes by putting the remaining three fingers of each hand on them. Making the humming sound in one exhalation is called one chakra (cycle) of Bhraamari Pranayam.

Duration: Practise 6-8 cycles of this pranayam.

Pace of Breathing: Inhale as much air as possible and exhale by making a low sound. Continue to breath in and out for a while.

Precautions: Keep your voice low and melodious.

Resolution: While doing this pranayam, imagine that your consciousness is being amalgamated with the cosmic consciousness and that the Almighty is showering blessings on you. Believe that the divine light is being kindled inside you, your ignorance is being dispelled, and you are being filled with emotions of love, friendship, compassion and joy.

Centre of Dhyan: Aajya Chakra.

Advantages: Bhraamari Pranayam removes mental fickleness and helps you overcome tension, anger, anxiety, frustration, depression, lack of sleep, confusion, laziness and migraine attacks. It also helps cure high blood pressure, cardiac diseases, throat ailments and rejuvenates the body.

Practise this aasan to get a vision of the divine light in Aajya Chakra. This makes the mind calm and introspective, helps in meditation and increases the memory.

SHAVAASAN

Procedure: Sit peacefully for some time after doing Bhraamari Pranayam. Then spread your legs apart from 1 to1.5ft, turn towards your left and lie on your back. Keep your hands on the ground, away from the body. Your palms should be half-open, facing the sky and you should close your eyes and lie like a corpse. Concentrate on your breathing. After that, shift your concentration to your body and try to feel every organ mentally.

Start from the toe and end at the head. This will relax all the organs and enable your body to go into the rest mode. After some time, bring your attention to the Aajya Chakra and try to concentrate inwards. After practising this exercise for a while, focus your attention on your breathing and inhale and exhale deeply, imagining that your body is being rejuvenated. Next, move the fingers of your hands and legs and rub the two palms together. When the palms become warm due to friction, keep them on your eyes. Remove the palms after a while, turn to the left and rise from this position. Sit in a meditative posture.

Advantages: This exercise cures physical and mental fatigue and rejuvenates the body and mind, making you feel happy and contented.

Pran Oorja Yog ends with this exercise.

After Shavaasan, close your eyes, chant *Aum* thrice and remember the Almighty. As you get up, convince yourself that the flow of Pran Oorja is increasing, making your body fit. To cure diseases, make this exercise part of your daily routine.

Pran Oorja Kriya

he mind is very fickle in nature and it's very difficult for it to remain at one place. It is observed that the mind is usually not where the body is. It keeps wandering on its own. It is not easy to control this fickle mind. It gets constantly influenced by our sensual and passionate desires and the environment. Hence, the wandering of the mind is the cause of our bondages. But, when the mind begins to look inwards and is self-conscious, it leads to liberation.

Yoga prescribes a few methods with which to make the mind (*mann*) *amann*, i.e. remove its fickleness.

A unique *kriya* has been developed by incorporating three different exercises, based on our experience and research. This new *kriya* has been named **Praan Oorja Kriya**. It's a three-minute exercise, based on breathing techniques and 'sakshibhav'; anyone can perform this exercise at any time of the day.

There is no doubt that every moment is precious in life. Even then a lot of time gets wasted every day. We can utilize that time by practicing Praan Oorja Kriya. The mind begins to become serene and inward looking; feelings of love, vigour, patience, concentration and memory also get a boost. Here, this exercise is described in brief. The whole exercise should be done with the eyes closed.

MINUTE 1:
CONCENTRATION ON BREATHING

Sit in a relaxed position. Keep the back and neck straight and close your eyes. Keep both the hands on your knees. Concentrate on your breathing for one minute and then start inhaling gradually to your capacity. Exhale gradually without holding the breath. Breath in and breath out in the same manner 5-6 times. It should be kept in mind that no sound should come out while breathing. As one deep breathing is done in 10-12 seconds, 5-6 cycles will take one minute.

MINUTE 2:
NAAD GUNJAN

After concentrating on breathing for a minute, do deep inhaling and exhaling in the second minute. Take out mild humming sound from the nostrils while breathing out. Repeat this process 5-6 times. Try to keep the humming sound as melodious as possible every time. Mind should concentrate on the humming sound while doing this exercise.

MINUTE 3:
AJAPA JAP

The mind attains serenity on its own after Naad Gunjan. Now, in the third *kriya,* concentrate on your normal inhalation and exhalation process and try to visualize those with a joyful mood. The pace of breathing should neither be increased nor decreased. Just feel the air going in and coming out. Try to notice minutely that a special sound is being produced while you are breathing in and breathing out. This is the *so-hum* sound. The *so* sound is produced when you breathe in and while breathing out, it sounds like *hum*. This is **Ajapa Jap** which happens 21,600 times in 24 hours but is not felt due to the outward inclination of our mind. But, once the mind is in peace, the flow of this sound can be heard with the help of our minute hearing power.

Get yourself immersed in Ajapa Jap after experiencing it for a while. Thereafter sit joyfully in the *dhyan* posture and feel that you are complete and brimming with love. Don't imagine anything at this stage, just be a mute witness to all that is happening in and around you. Think that what you are experiencing is 'for your self' only. That who was witness to the whole exercise were 'you' only. That who remained steadfast during the entire exercise were 'you' only. It was 'you' who experienced the inhalation and exhalation process, Naad Gunjan, the sound of *so-hum* etc. Sit in with this *saakshi bhaav,* peacefully for some time.

Thereafter, raise your hands and rub the palms vigorously. It will produce some heat. Put the palms, thus warmed, on the eyes. Remove the palms after some time and open the eyes.

The practitioner of Ajapa Jap remains immersed in it even when he performs his or her daily chores. Thus the practitioner feels liberated.

These combined exercises instill new energy in the mind and body. These exercises can be practised whenever one feels overpowered by tension, anger, annoyance, fear, exhaustion etc – at anytime of the day. One is able to experience sound sleep at night after doing this exercise. Tension will not affect you throughout the day if you practice these *kriya* in the morning.

Pran Oorja Kriya is especially useful for children as it increases their concentration powers and give a boost to memory. It can be practised in office to remove mental fatigue. Mental peace can be acquired by doing these *kriya* before worship, *dhyan* and yoga. Therefore this exercise can be done by any one, at any time of the day and anywhere. Many such benefits can be reaped by practising Pran Oorja Kriya.

Healthy Living

part from practising various kinds of yoga, there are certain rules and precautions that you should follow to ensure good health and increase your lifespan. You can regulate your life by adhering to them, and enhance the impact of yoga on your body. These are sure-fire ways to remain healthy.

GENERAL TIPS TO REMAIN HEALTHY

- Go to bed early and leave your bed before sunrise. Relieve yourself and then do Ushapaan. For **Ushapaan**, store some water in a copper utensil at night and drink two glasses of water from it in the morning. In winter, drink lukewarm water.
- Relieve yourself before sunrise and take deep breaths in the open.
- Make yoga a daily habit.
- Mould and regulate your life according to laws of nature because you cannot remain healthy by going against nature.
- Eat only when you are hungry and eat slightly less than required. Chew food well while eating and do not eat in between meals. Increase the intake of water and liquids like milk, buttermilk, soup and juice in your diet.
- Ensure that you eat food that is nutritious.

- Avoid food items that are extremely sweet, fried or spicy.
- In your daily routine, set aside some time for physical activities like walking, playing, climbing the ladder, doing exercises and engaging in household chores.
- Keep a fixed time for sleeping, waking up and eating. Take care to ensure cleanliness.
- Try to develop positive feelings of enthusiasm, self-control, balance, equality, satisfaction and love. Keep anger, stress, fear, irritation and jealousy at bay.
- If you persist in feeling that you are sick, you will unknowingly increase your chances of falling ill. Feeling good usually keeps a person physically fit. Therefore, always think that you are healthy and active.
- Do not allow the feeling that you are growing old to creep in or else you will unknowingly accelerate the ageing process.
- You should exercise control on your tongue and refrain from talking too much.
- Prevent your weight from increasing.
- *Aadhi* (mental disorder), *vyaadhi* (physical disorder) and *upadhi* (lust) are the greatest enemies of youth. Keep away from them.
- Ensure that you do not lose the habit of reading. Also, do not allow your brain to become slothful

or redundant. Do not let your nervous system become weak.

- Avoid smoking and drinking as they make you age faster.

USEFUL HEALTH-RELATED INFORMATION

- In case of any burning sensation in your eyes, keep some cold water in your mouth (don't swallow it) and then wash your eyes with cold water 15-20 times. Do this three to four times a day. Walk barefoot on green grass in the morning as it is beneficial for your eyes.
- Keeping a fat wallet in the rear pocket of a tight pair of trousers increases the risk of backache or sciatica.
- Apply some mustard oil in your nostrils before having a bath and wash your nose carefully after your bath. This prevents cough and cold.
- To ward off cough and cold during winter, cover your ears before leaving the bed and wear slippers as soon as you get down from bed.
- You can reduce fat in your body by rubbing and massaging it while having a bath.
- If you massage your body with mustard oil for five minutes every day before your bath, you can keep your body fit and the skin soft.
- To ensure sound sleep at night, wash your feet properly and massage them with mustard oil before going to bed.
- Practise Bhraamari Pranayam regularly to cure sleeplessness.
- Close your eyes and try to recount your daily activities. This will increase your memory.
- Soak five almonds in water overnight. Peel their skin in the morning and eat them to improve your memory.
- Sit in Vajrasan for 10 minutes after your meals. It helps improve your digestion and cures constipation, gas and flatulence. However, those suffering from pain in the knees should not do this aasan.
- If you feel uneasy after over-eating, practise Vajrasan.
- Refrain from eating curd at night to minimize chances of arthritis, gout and gas.
- Gently massage your gums and teeth, using the middle finger of the right hand in the morning to make them strong.
- Cleaning the palate with the right thumb after brushing your teeth in the morning prevents hairfall and cough and cold.
- Before going to sleep at night, apply mustard oil in your navel to prevent cracking of lips.
- If you drink milk along with mutton, chicken, fish, salted snacks and sour items, you'll become susceptible to skin diseases.
- Children who start speaking late or speak less should be made to drink more water.
- Drinking water in a single gulp increases chances of cough. You should take long sips of water instead of gulping it.
- Go to the toilet after meals, before having a bath and before going to bed.
- In order to invigorate the body, inhale and exhale deeply while walking.
- Don't drink cold water, ice cream or soft drinks immediately after eating hot food. It weakens

the teeth and has a bad impact on digestive organs.

- If you have a backache, lie straight, roll a towel and place it at the point where the pain is maximum. Lie in Shavaasan for 10-15 minutes.
- Food that is very sour can affect the throat. While food high in sugar content can cause blood-related disorders, excessive intake of salt can harm the kidneys. Too much of *maida* (refined flour) in your food can trigger stomach disorders.
- Always sit with your back and neck straight. It improves the flow of energy in your body, removes lethargy, increases enthusiasm and keeps the body healthy.
- Let your face exude happiness throughout the day. Laugh aloud every time you get an opportunity to do so.
- Pull your ears and massage the area near them to get relief from headaches.
- Sufficient intake of water flushes impurities from the body and makes it light and fresh.
- Turn to your left while sitting or lying to avoid putting pressure on your waist and heart.
- Soak two pods of garlic in water overnight. Cut and swallow them with a glass of fresh water to cure rheumatism.
- Eat a clove or a small piece of *gur* (jaggery) to curb acidity
- Grind five basil leaves, five peppercorns, five neem leaves and five bael leaves and make globules out of them. Take these globules early in the morning on an empty stomach to control diabetes.

- In case of aches and pain in your legs, massage the region below the calf and near the ankle when you have a bath. This will provide relief to the entire body.
- Put a piece of camphor in coconut oil and place it in the sun for a while. Massage this oil on your body to get relief from eczema, dandruff and itching. It is also beneficial to boil 8-10 neem leaves in water and use that water for bathing.
- To get relief from migraine attacks, put 3-4 drops of ghee (prepared from cow's milk) into both your nostrils before going to bed at night.
- Don't have apples, fruit juice or milk on an empty stomach in the morning if you are suffering from gas.
- Add rock salt and powdered dry ginger to buttermilk if you are suffering from dysentery or diarrhoea.
- You can keep high blood pressure under control by drinking lemon water 3-4 times a day.
- Make a powdered mixture of pepper, dry ginger, *pipli* (long pepper) and liquorice, keeping the ingredients in equal proportion. Take a quarter spoon of this mixture with honey to cure cough and cold.
- While sleeping, do not keep your head towards the north. It increases the possibility of mental disorder.
- Relieve yourself twice a day, in the morning and evening, to prevent constipation. Make this a daily habit.
- While sitting on a chair, keep one leg before the other, to prevent stretching the waist.
- If you use thick pillows and soft mattresses for

sleeping, it may cause pain in the backbone.

- To cure any ache in the body, lie in Shavaasan and take a deep breath gradually. Direct Pran Vayu to the spot that is paining and imagine that it is being cured.
- Increase your intake of liquids on days when you fast. Refrain from eating heavy, difficult-to-digest food like *puri, parantha* and *kachauri* to break your fast.
- Clench your teeth and jaws tightly while relieving yourself. It makes the teeth strong.
- To protect yourself from heatwave while going out in summers, cover your ears with cloth and drink plenty of water.
- If you have a running nose caused by exposure to cold winds, put some cotton wads in your ears and muffle your head while sleeping.
- If your leg becomes numb by sitting in the same position for a long period, you can get relief by pulling the ear on the opposite side of the body.

DO NOT SUPPRESS NATURAL URGES

- Do not suppress natural urges or postpone relieving yourself. It can lead to several disorders.

- Putting off defecation results in abdominal pain, constipation, gas and flatulence. It also makes the blood impure.
- Putting off urination causes pain in the bladder and urethra and makes a person restless.
- Restricting the flow of semen may cause pain and swelling in the abdomen, scrotum, kidney and bladder.
- By putting off belching, you may feel a sense of heaviness in the chest, your stomach may rumble and you may experience uneasiness in the neck.
- Putting off a sneeze may cause pain in the neck and head, migraine attacks and mental disorders. It may also weaken various organs of the body.
- Putting off vomiting may cause blood-related disorders, swelling, inflammation of the liver, eczema, heaviness in the chest and loss of appetite.
- Putting off Apaan Vaayu may cause swelling of the stomach, fatigue, stomach ache, problem in urinating and defecating.
- Putting off or postponing sleep causes pain in the head and eyes, yawning, heaviness, indigestion and constipation.

Daily Routine

person should follow a regulated routine in order to enjoy good health. Ayurveda has prescribed an ideal daily regimen for us. Described below is the routine in today's context.

Activities — right from waking up in the morning to going to bed at night — that ensure good health, should make up your daily routine. You should get up before *brahmamuhurtha* (daybreak) after a refreshing sleep and start your day by taking stock of whether the meal you ate the night before has been properly digested or not. If you want to ease yourself, do so. Otherwise, you should just brush your teeth and drink water kept in a copper utensil. If the weather is cold, you should have warm water. Drinking this water clears the oesophagus and intestine and helps in defecating and urinating. It is unwise to apply pressure while defecating as it can lead to piles. While relieving yourself, press the teeth of both jaws against each other. After this, clean your teeth with datoon or toothbrush, taking care to use good toothpowder or toothpaste. Clean your tongue with a tongue cleaner and your palate with the right thumb. Gargle and then wash your eyes and face thoroughly. Next, get on with your exercises.

EXERCISE

This is essential for keeping your body healthy, carrying out daily chores efficiently and rejuvenating yourself. If you don't exercise, your body will become weak and you will get exhausted quickly. A regular exercise regimen will increase your energy, strengthen your muscles and bones, improve your appetite and remove toxic foreign elements from your body. It will also increase the circulation of blood and oxygen in your body, make you more active and enable the organs of the body to function properly. You will feel full of energy and vigour.

Yoga acquires a prominent place among various exercises. It keeps your body fit, rejuvenates the mind and can cure any disease. As yoga results in all-round development, you should practise it for half an hour to one hour daily and follow it up with a body massage.

MASSAGE

A regular application of oil on the body during massage keeps old age, fatigue and mental disorders at bay. Apart from ensuring sound sleep, it makes the skin glow. For massage, you should use oil according to the time of the year. In winters, the oil that you use should warm the body, while in summers the oil used should have a cooling effect. In order to improve the flow of blood to the heart, massage should be done from the lower part of the body to the upper part. Legs, head and ears should be massaged as well. The acupressure points of the body are automatically pressed and keep the body healthy. The massage should be done for five to ten minutes.

Take a bath only when the body regains its normal temperature.

BATH

Have a bath daily with clean and fresh water. The temperature of the water should be according to the season. A bath cleans the body and removes fatigue, perspiration, itching and dryness. Together with a feeling of freshness and happiness, a bath improves blood circulation and increases the appetite.

Except for persons who are ill, everyone should have a bath with fresh water. In case of severe cold, you may use warm water. Rub and massage the entire body while bathing and use sufficient quantity of water. After your bath, dry your body properly with a clean towel. This brisk act of drying up also helps to reduce extra flab from the body. While having a bath, chant God's name and imagine that along with the dirt from the body, your negative thoughts too are being washed away. After your bath, it is a good practice to touch the feet of elders in the house and seek their blessings.

PRAYER

After having a bath, you can sit in a meditative posture for a while. Chanting mantras, engaging in *jap* (chanting), singing *bhajans*, participating in *satsang* and visiting a temple — all these make up prayer.

BREAKFAST

After the prayers, eat a fresh and nutritious breakfast. You can have milk, porridge, fruits, sprouted grains or other light and healthy food items. Avoid heavy food like *paranthas*, *pakoras*, bread and items made from *maida* as they adversely affect the digestive system.

WORK

After this, you should go to work and do your job sincerely. While working, thank the Almighty that he has given you an opportunity to serve humanity.

MEALS

Eat a healthy and nutritious lunch at around 1pm and continue with your daily activities. It is not healthy to sleep in the afternoon although you may take a short nap if you are feeling very tired. Eat your dinner by 8pm and sit in Vajraasan for 10-15 minutes. You should retire to bed two hours after dinner, i.e. by 10pm.

Be happy throughout the day. Whenever and wherever you sit, try to keep your back and neck straight. Walk for sometime in the morning and evening, breathing deeply, and don't think anything at that time. Don't talk to anyone while walking. Concentrate on your body and keep thinking that it is becoming healthy. Walk amidst trees, plants and flowers, seek energy from nature and become one with it.

SLEEP

Sleep is essential for good health and lack of it may lead to several disorders. When the sense organs and the mind get exhausted, you go into a state of slumber. In the yogic discipline, it is believed that when the body is overwhelmed with **Tama gun**, i.e. the quality of *tama* or darkness and ignorance, we fall asleep. When **Sattva gun**, i.e. the quality of purity and goodness, is dominant, we are awake. Sometimes, the body is exhausted but the mind remains connected to the external world. In such a condition, you may go to sleep but will have various kinds of dreams.

Sound sleep will bring about physical well-being and mental happiness, rejuvenate the senses, sharpen your mental abilities and heighten your ability to concentrate. It can also increase your lifespan. In keeping with the law of nature, rise before daybreak, work during the day and go to bed early at night. Any other routine can cause various ailments.

Waste Material of the Body

The human body is made up of *Panchtattva* (five elements) — earth, water, fire, air and space. These elements keep the body toned and healthy. When either of these elements become weak or are defiled by the waste material they produce, we fall ill. Each element has its specific work and that leads to the formation of a certain kind of waste material. If this waste continues to remain in the body, it can cause diseases. It is, therefore, imperative to expel waste products from the body.

By relieving yourself in the morning, you throw out waste material from the body. Excreta is waste material produced by the element earth. Similarly, urine is refuse discharged by the element water. After relieving yourself in the morning, you should practise aasan, Pranayam or other exercises to keep your body fit and discharge carbon dioxide — waste material produced by the element air — from the body. Similarly, bad and offending heat of the body, which is a waste material of the element fire, is washed away when we take a bath. The waste material of the element space — negative thoughts — is dispelled from the body when we worship, attend *satsang* or practise meditation. The body can be kept healthy by discharging waste material produced by the five elements of the body in the morning. If any one of these waste materials remains in the body, we may fall sick.

If the refuse of the element earth is not expelled from the body, it may lead to constipation, indigestion, gas, loss of appetite, belching, obesity, piles, blood impurities, skin diseases, fatigue, depression, joint pain, headache, weak eyesight, diabetes, high blood pressure, hair-related problems, nocturnal emission and impotency. Similarly, if the refuse of the element water, i.e. urine, remains in the body, it increases the level of toxic substances in it. It causes diseases of the kidney and bladder. If a person does not bathe, the refuse of the element fire is not expelled from the body. So, it causes burning and itching in the body, foul sweat and reduces immunity. It results in skin diseases, loss of appetite and lack of freshness. If one doesn't do aasans, Pranayam or any other exercise, waste matter of the element air will remain in the body and may cause respiratory diseases, asthma, cardiac problems, skin diseases and kidney disorders. If you neither meditate nor attend *satsang*, the refuse of the element air will become stagnant in the mind. It will then lead to negative thoughts, tension, worry, depression, high blood pressure, anxiety, anger, insomnia, mental fickleness, dissatisfaction and inflated ego.

Thus, the main reason for most of our diseases is the accumulated waste material. No disease exists in isolation, for one leads to the other. To ensure a disease-free body, you should prevent all waste matter from remaining in it.

Diet

The natural state of the body is to be free of diseases and stay healthy. Good health is a gift of the Almighty. Violation of the laws of nature leads to diseases, disorders, aches and weaknesses. These are unnatural states of the body and mind. Usually, persons who lead a life not in consonance with nature or are inclined towards physical pleasures become careless about their health. This often leads to various kinds of diseases. Improper diet is a vital reason behind this.

Food, sleep and *brahmacharya* (control over sexual urges) are the three pillars of human life. Defining food, Maharshi Charak had said, *Aahiyate annanalikaya yattadaharah*. He described food as that significant material that is transported to the stomach by the food pipe, nourishes the organs, regulates various activities of the body and helps in the growth of various organs.

MODERATION IN DIET

According to Ayurveda, *yukta aahar* (proper food) ensures the health and growth of the body, while *ayukta aahar* (improper food) can cause diseases. While eating, moderation in diet is recommended. One should eat according to the place, time, season, one's physical condition, mental inclination and profession. Only then is the body's equilibrium maintained and its various organs, including the excretory system, are in perfect condition. A moderate diet keeps you in good humour:

Susnigdhamadhuraharaschaturthansh vivarjitah
Bhujyate shivasamprityyai mitaharah sa uchyate
(Hathyog Pradipika, 1/58)

This *sutra* means that the food you eat should be soft and sweet and should be taken in the name of the Almighty. Eat only that much quantity of food that fills three-fourths of your stomach. One-fourth of the stomach should be left empty for the digestion process and air. Therefore, always eat slightly less than your appetite. *Hatha Pradipika* gives the following description about the kind of food you should eat:

Pushtamsumadhuramshigdham gavyam dhaatu
praposhnam
Mahobhilashitam yogyam yogi bhojanamacharet.
(Hathyog Pradipika,1/63)

This means that food should be nutritious, tasty and easy to digest. It should invariably contain milk products and essential nutrients for physical and mental growth.

Significantly, food is not only a means of filling your stomach or satisfying your hunger, but a basic ingredient that makes up the seven essential elements of the body — fluid, blood, flesh, fat, bone, bone marrow and sperm. Food provides energy to various organs of the body and keeps it healthy. Therefore, you should be careful while deciding what you eat and should ensure that your food includes carbohydrate, fat, protein, vitamins, minerals, salt and water. The food you eat should contain all the six *rasa*s (tastes/flavours) — sweet, sour, salty, bitter, hot and pungent — and should be of all colours.

CHEW PROPERLY

Don't eat in a hurry. Eat slowly and happily with the implicit belief that the food is enhancing your energy, intelligence, age and health. Every morsel you take should be chewed thoroughly. We usually chew food only about 7-8 times or till it retains its taste in the mouth. Because of this, saliva doesn't mix properly with the food and the intestine has to put in extra effort to digest the half-chewed food. This makes the intestine and teeth weak. Proper chewing ensures better absorption of essential nutrients. Make a paste of the food before swallowing it and drink liquids in small sips.

Don't drink water while eating. If the food you are eating is dry and you want to drink water, take it in sips to aid digestion. Ideally, drink water either half an hour before meals or one hour after meals.

THE TONGUE

The tongue performs two functions — tasting and talking. You can always remain healthy and happy if you control these two activities. It is when you lose control over your tongue that you get tempted to eat junk food and fall ill. Similarly, when your tongue gets out of control, you become nasty in your speech. If you regularly eat spicy and fried food items for breakfast, lunch and dinner, you become a slave of your tongue and your health gets affected. To ensure good health, assess the quality and nature of food before you eat it. If you exercise restraint on your tongue, most of your health problems will be resolved.

PROXIMITY TO NATURE

By being close to nature, you remain healthy. When you move away from nature, you compound your health problems. Therefore, by tapping the benefits of nature, you stand to gain. While eating, you should opt for seasonal vegetables and fruits, grain and dried fruits. Food that is kept in cold storage loses its nutritional value.

Traditionally, Indians use their hands to eat. But because of increasing Westernization, many people have started using spoons, knives and forks. When you eat food with a spoon, the mouth does not automatically release saliva. But when you eat with your hand, as soon as you put food in your mouth, it triggers the release of saliva, which helps to digest food. This acts as a catalyst in digestion. A person who eats with a spoon doesn't have this advantage.

LACK OF EMOTIONAL ATTACHMENT WITH DIET

Some people think that the period spent eating is a waste of time. They prefer to read books, newspapers or watch television while eating. Though they feel that they have utilized their time well, they fail to realize that they are harming their health owing to lack of any emotional attachment with what they are eating. When we are indifferent to the benefits of eating food, our diet fails to provide energy to our body or help us develop immunity to diseases. Such people complain of not feeling healthy despite eating nutritious food. While eating, you should keep your mind peaceful and focus only on food. During meals, refrain from anger, irritation, haste and negative thinking. Whoever cooks the food should also think that the person who eats it will derive strength, intelligence and longevity from it. To guard against diseases, pay attention to cleanliness and the quality of food while cooking and during its consumption.

RELATIONSHIP BETWEEN TONGUE AND BODY

The food you eat should not only appeal to your taste buds but should also ensure good health. Often, we prefer a diet that satisfies our tongue even if it makes us prone to diseases. Snacking frequently has its disadvantages because it hampers digestion. According to Ayurveda, there should be a gap of at least three hours between meals but this gap should not stretch beyond six hours. If you remain without food for a long time, it may result in several disorders.

RELIEVE YOURSELF TWICE A DAY

As lunch and dinner make up your main meals, you should relieve yourself twice a day. Most people defecate only once a day, leaving excreta lying in the intestine. This results in constipation, a feeling of heaviness, giddiness, impurity in the blood, skin diseases and flatulence. Hence, you should relieve yourself in the morning and then before dinner.

YOUR DIET SHOULD BE IN TANDEM WITH NATURE

Ailments of Vaat, Pitta and Kapha — which are always present in our body — cause a number of diseases. We should choose a diet in accordance with the nature of our body and its ailments. If you suffer from Vaat ailments, avoid sour food like curd, buttermilk, *kadhi-chawal* and items like *arvi*, okra, rajma, chana dal and urad dal. Those afflicted with ailments relating to Pitta should not eat food that generates heat like tea, coffee, spices and oily items. Those who suffer from Kapha should avoid rice, curd, milk, ice cream and refrigerated food.

PROPER AND IMPROPER FOOD

Roughly, food can be divided into two categories — *pathya* (proper food) and *apathya* (improper food). Food items that enhance your physical and mental strength and increase your lifespan come under proper food. And food items that cause diseases in the body are bracketed under improper food. We should be conscious about what we eat. Bhagavad Gita describes three categories of food on the basis of their virtues and vices — **Saatvik**, **Raajsik** and **Taamsik**. The nature of people plays a decisive role in the particular type of food that they like.

Saatvik Food: This food enhances longevity, physical and mental health and ensures peace of mind. Such food items are juicy, smooth in texture and remain in the body for a longer period of time.

Saatvik or virtuous people like this kind of food.

Raajsik Food: Raajsik food items are bitter, hot, sour, salty, weight inducing and often cause anxiety or unhappiness. People with royal taste like Raajsik food.

Taamsik Food: Taamsik food is semi-cooked, juiceless, stale, foul-smelling and unhygienic.

FOOD COMBINATIONS

Some food items work like ambrosia when eaten on their own, but act like poison when mixed with other eatables.

- Don't take the following items with milk: curd, salt, tamarind, musk melon, coconut, radish, radish leaves, *tori*, *tilkut*, *kulthi*, *sattoo* and sour items.
- Eating the following items with curd can be injurious to health: milk, *kheer*, *paneer*, musk melon and hot substances.

- Do not eat radish and grapes with honey.
- Refrain from eating *khichri*, sour substances, *sattoo* and jackfruit with *kheer*.
- Avoid taking groundnuts, guavas, cucumber, blackberries, watermelon, ghee, oil, hot milk and other hot food with cold water.
- If you eat radish leaves, milk, curd and garlic with watermelon, it can be injurious to your health.
- Don't take tea with cucumber.
- Avoid the following combinations: rice with vinegar and watermelon with *pudina* (mint) and cold water.

Certain combinations can, however, be beneficial for health. For example, date palm with milk; rice with curd; mango with cow's milk; cardamom with banana; musk melon with sugar; rice with coconut; tamarind with jaggery; guava with fennel seeds; corn with buttermilk and *bathua* with curd.

Tridosh

Tridosh, a basic principle of Ayurveda, refers to the three doshas of vayu, pitta and kapha. These doshas have two stages — even and uneven. In the even stage, Tridosh is balanced, in a natural state and ensures the body's health. In the uneven stage, the dosha loses its balance, causing diseases.

If, in the initial stage, the disease is left untreated, it may become serious. Therefore, to keep your body healthy and free of ailments, you should lead your life carefully, so that the three doshas remain balanced.

To ensure that the three doshas are balanced, Ayurveda prescribes six types of *rasas* in your diet — sour, sweet, salty, bitter, pungent and astringent. Sweet, sour and salty food increase cough. Bitter, salty and sour food increase bile, while bitter, pungent and astringent food increase wind in the body. Food items that increase cough in the body either reduce or pacify the wind. Sweet, bitter and astringent food items control bile while bitter, pungent and astringent food reduce cough.

VAAT DOSH

Vaat is arid, minute, fickle, cooling and healing. Having features of Raja Guna, it is considered to be the strongest among the three doshas. Pitta and kapha would be unable to function in the absence of Vaat for Vaat Dosh separates all materials, including excreta, and enables the body to carry out its activities. Life exists because of Vaat, which is of five types — **Udanvaayu**, **Pranvaayu**, **Samanvaayu**, **Apaanvaayu** and **Vyaanvaayu**.

Symptoms of Vaat fury: Physical symptoms of an imbalance of vaat are stiffness, strain, weakness, numbness and dryness in the body. Vaat, when imbalanced, causes pain and aches in joints; discomfort in the body; shivering, gas, hiccups, belching, farting, dryness in the mouth, hoarseness, cracking of lips and palms, lack of appetite and constipation. These lead to exhaustion and loss of sleep. In extreme cases, it also results in loss of hearing, weakening of the nervous system, paralysis, arthritis, sciatica and back pain. According to Ayurveda, the fury of Vaat may cause up to eighty kinds of diseases.

Vaat is usually in its most virulent form between 2pm and 6pm and between 2am and 6am after the digestion of meals. The situation aggravates when winds blow, in cold climate, in an arid environment and when the sky is overcast. Problems connected with Vaat often become acute in old age.

Remedial Measures: An effective remedy to counter an imbalance of vaat is to take sweet, sour and salty food. Eat chapattis made of wheat flour, kulthi, mustard, ginger, onion, mint, *bathua*, gourd, parwal, radish, carrot, drumstick, grapes, orange, papaya, mango, pomegranate and dates.

When your body is troubled by wind disorders, it is beneficial to have an oil massage. However, the oil used for massage (almond oil, mustard oil), should be chosen according to the prevailing season. When you are afflicted by an imbalance of vaat, ensure that you do not have constipation. Drink water frequently and have bath in tepid water. Drinking warm water is also helpful.

PITTA DOSH

Pitta is yellow, smooth, thin, purgative and pungent in taste. By nature, it has characteristics of Sattva Guna. Pitta is considered to be of five types — **Pachak** (digestive), **Ranjak** (colouring), **Saadhak** (effective), **Alochak** (critical) and **Bhrajak** (gleaming).

Symptoms of Pitta Dosh: When pitta is imbalanced, your entire body, including stomach, oesophagus, throat and chest, start burning; you have boils on the skin; you feel very hot; your throat becomes parched and everything tastes bitter. In this condition, the skin and eyes become yellowish and so does the colour of the excreta and urine. You may also suffer from vomiting, headaches, jaundice or diarrhoea. A person with pitta disorder may also suffer from sleeplessness, excess perspiration and rapid pulse. According to Ayurveda, a pitta disorder may cause forty types of diseases. An excess of pitta generally peaks in the afternoon, two hours after eating your meals, and when you eat food that is hot. It is most active in autumn.

Remedial measures: If you suffer from pitta disorder, eating the right kind of food will provide you relief. You should eat food that is sweet, bitter, cold and astringent. You should have barley, wheat, millet, sattoo, moong, cow's milk, cream, curd with sugar, pudding, bitter gourd, parwal, bathua, coriander, mint, cabbage, watermelon, amla, banana, coconut, apple, plum, pomegranate, raisins, lemon soda, buttermilk before lunch, saunf after meals, clove, jaggery, cardamom, turmeric, vegetable soup, fruit juice and isabgol. Applying sandal paste on the neck and forehead, drinking cold milk and cold water, relaxing in a moonlit night and massaging coconut oil or ghee made of cow's milk are beneficial.

KAPHA DOSH

Kapha is greasy, clammy, heavy, cool and salty in nature. It has characteristics of Tama Guna. In Ayurveda, five types of kapha have been described — **Khedan, Avalamban, Rasan, Snehan** and **Shleshma**.

Symptoms Of Kapha Disorder: When you suffer from Kapha Dosh, your body becomes heavy and you feel cold. Some prominent symptoms of Kapha disorders are loss of appetite, weakness, exhaustion, laziness, feeling of sweetness in the mouth, excess secretion of saliva, whitening of eyes and body, whitening of excreta and urine and diarrhoea. According to Ayurveda, Kapha Dosh may cause about twenty diseases and usually occurs between 6am and 10am, immediately after meals and during indigestion. It peaks during spring.

Remedial Measures: Eating food that is bitter, pungent and astringent; food that reduces extra flab; chapattis made from wheat and barley; gram; moong; barley; mustard oil; kulthi; goat's milk; buttermilk; fresh honey; carrot; garlic; cucumber; bathua; ginger; onion; bitter gourd; dry fruits; bael fruit; watermelon; apple; pomegranate; pepper; clove; turmeric; neem leaves; basil leaves; *saunf*; *triphala*; carom seeds and asafoetida prove beneficial. Vomiting, performing Neti Kriya and perspiring also help. To get relief, you can have an early dinner, keep fasts, exercise regularly, drink warm water, take bath in tepid water, avoid dampness in winter and bask in the sun to cure any cough-related disorder. Also, refrain from sleeping during the day.

Hasta Mudras

Our body in itself is a mystery. The power and ability to stay healthy lies within. The only thing the body is required to do is to understand, organize and balance its power. The body is made up of five basic elements and can remain fit and free of ailments only if all five are balanced.

According to the treatment by hand postures, the five fingers of a hand represent the five elements. Each finger empowers its corresponding element through cosmic energy. The thumb represents fire, the index finger air, the middle finger space, the ring finger earth and the little finger water. You can make mudras (hand postures) by joining the fingers.

Mudras immediately start showing their effect. Sit in any meditative posture like Padmaasan, Swastikaasan, Sukhaasan or Vajraasan to practise the mudras. Now, make the relevant hand posture with the implicit belief that it will cure your disease. This positive feeling enhances the effect of the posture. Practise each mudra for 10 to 15 minutes to derive maximum benefit. If it is not possible to do it in a single sitting, the mudra can be practised in two or three parts. In any mudra, keep those fingers that are not used straight, the palm slightly tight and the rest of the hand loose. Although there are many hand postures, the important ones are described here:

GYAN MUDRA

Method: Join the tips of the thumbs of both your hands with the respective index fingers, while other fingers remain straight. Keep both hands on your knees, with the palms facing upwards. Sit in a meditative posture, keeping the neck and back straight and the eyes closed.

Advantages: This posture empowers nerves of the brain and improves your memory, concentration and resolve. It also increases intelligence, cures sleeplessness and headaches and removes mental fickleness. Gyan Mudra helps to fight fretfulness, tension and anxiety and guides you towards spirituality.

VAYU MUDRA
Method: Fold the index fingers of both the hands and press them slightly at the base of the respective thumbs. Keep your hands on the knees, with the palms facing upwards. Sit in a meditative posture, keeping your neck and back straight, and eyes closed.

Advantages: Vayu Mudra is especially beneficial in Vaat-related diseases. It pacifies an angry mind and provides relief in sciatica, pain in the waist or neck, Parkinson's disease, arthritis, paralysis, knee and joint aches.

AKASH MUDRA
Method: Touch the tip of the thumbs with your middle fingers; keep other fingers straight. Now, keep your hands on your knees, with your palms facing upwards. Sit in a meditative position, keeping the neck and back straight, and the eyes closed.

Advantages: Akash Mudra helps to address loss of hearing and other diseases of the ear and helps cure bone-related disorders.

SHUNYA MUDRA

Method: Fold the middle finger of both the hands and press them at the base of the respective thumbs. Now, keep your hands on your knees, with your palms facing upwards. Sit in a meditative position, keeping the neck and back straight and eyes closed.

Advantages: Shunya Mudra is beneficial in curing problems of the neck and disorders of the thyroid gland. It makes your teeth strong and cures ailments of the ear.

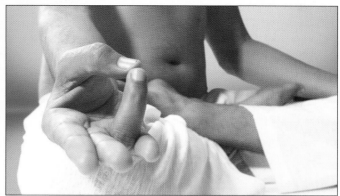

PRITHVI MUDRA

Method: Bring the ring finger of both your hands to the tips of the respective thumbs, keeping the other fingers straight. Now, keep your hands on the knees, with palms facing upwards. Sit in a meditative position, keeping the neck and back straight and eyes closed.

Advantages: Prithvi Mudra cures weakness, helps to

put on weight and increases physical strength. It makes you active, brings a glow to your face and increases the life force. It also strengthens your digestive system.

SURYA MUDRA

Method: Bring the ring fingers of both your hands to the base of the respective thumbs. Now, press both

these fingers with the thumbs in such a way that other fingers remain straight. Keep your hands on your knees, with the palms facing upwards. Sit in a meditative posture, keeping the neck and back straight and your eyes closed.

Advantages: This mudra checks obesity and helps you shed extra weight. It gives warmth to the body, increases physical strength and keeps the cholesterol under control. It is also beneficial in diabetes and liver disorders.

Note: A weak person should not practise this mudra. It should also be done sparingly in summer.

VARUN MUDRA

Method: Bring the little fingers of both hands to the tips of the respective thumbs. Keep other fingers straight. Now, keep your hands on the knees, with the palms facing upwards. Sit in a meditative position, keeping the neck and back straight, and eyes closed.

Advantages: This mudra cures skin diseases and impurities of the blood. It is beneficial for dry skin and makes it soft and glowing. It improves the complexion.

Note: Persons susceptible to cough and cold should not practise this mudra.

APAAN MUDRA

Method: Bring the middle and ring fingers of both your hands to the tips of the respective thumbs. Keep other fingers straight. Now, keep your hands on the knees, with the palms facing upwards. Sit in a meditative position, keeping the neck and back straight and eyes closed.

Advantages: Apaan Mudra helps in curing constipation, diabetes, kidney disorders, flatulence and piles. As a result, you perspire and urinate more than before. The mudra cleanses the body, removes disorders in the naadis, eradicates blockages in the urinary tract and makes teeth strong.

HRIDAYA MUDRA

Method: Bring the index fingers of both the hands to the respective thumbs and let the middle and ring fingers touch the tips of the two thumbs. Keep the little finger straight. Now, keep your hands on the knees, with your palms facing upwards. Sit in a

meditative position, keeping the neck and back straight and eyes closed.

Advantages: This mudra is especially beneficial for cardiac diseases. Practice it for 10-15 minutes every day to make your heart strong and to prevent gas, headaches, asthma and high blood pressure. If you adopt this mudra before climbing stairs, you will not suffer from breathlessness.

LING MUDRA

Method: Fold the elbows and interlock the fingers of both your hands with the thumb of the left hand erect. Sit in a meditative position, keeping the neck and back straight and eyes closed.

Advantages: This mudra has a warming effect on the body. It is beneficial when you have cough and cold, sinusitis, asthma and low blood pressure.

Note: This mudra should not be practised unless required.

99

Mystery of Yoga

THREE GUNAS

Sattva, Rajas and Tama are considered to be the three constituents of nature. According to Sankhya philosophy, the imbalance of these three elements brought the cosmos into being. From time immemorial, these three elements have been imbedded in nature. As a result, every matter in this world has at least one of these three gunas. The entire creation comes into being, sustains itself and, finally, gets destroyed due to the combination and separation of these interdependent elements. When Sattva Guna dominates, the other two gunas become subdued. Similarly, when Sattva and Rajas Gunas become docile, Tama Guna dominates. Sometimes, Rajas Guna dominates, rendering Sattva Guna and Tama Guna docile. In fact, our behaviour changes according to the guna that is dominant.

1. **Sattva Guna:** This guna is light, refreshing and enlightening, and reflects similar traits when it dominates. A person with Sattva Guna is filled with zeal, enthusiasm, happiness and contentment. He feels light and refreshed physically and mentally whenever the Sattva Guna in him dominates. Just as fire ascends upwards owing to its light weight, the dominance of Sattva Guna helps a person ascend in life and makes him responsible. Sattva Guna is associated with white colour. In nature, Sattva Guna is dominant during daybreak.

2. **Rajas Guna:** The characteristics of Rajas Guna are excitement, fickleness of mind and suffering. The mobility and fickleness of air is due to the presence of Rajas Guna in it. This guna makes sense organs attracted to objects of desire. When Rajas Guna dominates in a person, he gets excited and his mind starts wandering. This leads to suffering. It is Rajas Guna that inspires Sattva Guna and Tama Guna to perform their actions. Only Rajas Guna is action oriented and inspires you to engage in work; the other two gunas are activated by it. The colour red is associated with Rajas Guna, which is active during the day.

3. **Tama Guna:** This guna is weighty, alluring and brings hurdles in life. It is the opposite of Sattva Guna and is the symbol of inertness and inactivity. Tama Guna reduces the brilliance of a person's mind and spurs him on to careless acts. The dominance of Tama Guna results in laziness, giddiness and passion and makes one lose interest in work. It also prevents a person from gaining knowledge. Black is the colour of Tama Guna, which becomes dominant at night.
   In spite of being contradictory in nature, the three gunas work in unison.

THE FIVE STATES OF MIND

1. **Moodhavastha:** Dominance of Tama Guna brings about this state. Sattva and Rajas Gunas remain dormant in this state, which is triggered by passion, anger, lust, greed and possessiveness. In this state, a person is inclined towards sin, ignorance, nihilism and desire. This state of mind gives rise to meanness.

2. **Khshiptavasthaa:** This state of mind is due to the dominance of Rajas Guna, in which Tama and Sattva Gunas remain dormant. This state is brought about by feelings of love or hatred. A person in Khshiptavasthaa is often inclined or attracted towards contradictory forces like religion or sin, love or hate, attachment or renunciation, knowledge or ignorance. Thus, when Sattva Guna overpowers Rajas Guna, the mind is inclined towards religion, love, attachment and knowledge. When Rajas Guna overpowers Sattva Guna, the opposite happens.

3. **Vikshiptavastha:** Dominance of Sattva Guna over Rajas Guna and Tama Guna brings about this state. Vikshiptavastha is attained by abandoning feelings of love and hate, passion and anger, greed and possessiveness and by working without desire. In this state, a person is inclined towards religion, knowledge, affluence and asceticism, but he often goes insane due to the presence of Rajas Guna. Highly intellectual and inquisitive people usually go into this state of mind. But in spite of being an elevated state of mind, this is not a normal state because the mind is influenced by many external factors.

4. **Ekagravastha:** When thought is focused on a single subject, the state of mind is called Ekagravastha. It is a natural state of mind in which there is no influence of external factors. Ekagravastha — in which the mind becomes completely pure — is achieved by constant practice of dhyaan or meditation. In yoga, this state is also called Sampragyat Samadhi. The practitioner interacts with forces of nature, becomes discerning and appreciates the difference between mind and *aatman*.

5. **Niruddhavastha:** A practitioner achieves Niruddhavastha after Ekagravastha by rigorous practice. After reaching this stage, he develops a special kind of asceticism, referred to as a satiric trait or condition of the mind. He gets attached to this trait and either negates or restricts the possibilities of asceticism. Thus, after negating or controlling all hindrances, he reaches the stage of Niruddhavastha where all acquired and communicated *sanskaaras* are destroyed. Hence, it is also called **Nirbeej** or **Asampragyat Samadhi**. In this condition, a person stays in his original state. This is called nihilism, **kaivalya**, **moksha** or yog.

ELEMENTS THAT HINDER AND FACILITATE YOGA

Factors that prevent a yoga practitioner from achieving his goal are known as hindering elements while those that enable a *saadhak* to achieve success in yogic pursuit are called facilitating elements. These have been described separately in Hathyog and Patanjali Yog.

ELEMENTS HINDERING YOGA ACCORDING TO HATHYOG

Hathyog Pradipika has described elements hindering the practice of yoga in the following extract:

Atyaharaha Prayasascha Prajalponiyamgreha
Janasangascha laulyam cha shadbhiryogo vinashyati

(*Hathyog Pradipika* 1/15)

This means that *atyaahar* (over-eating), *prayas* (perseverance), *prajalpa* (distraction), *niyamgraha* (violation of rules), *jansang* (interaction with people) and *chanchalta* (fickleness of mind) are six things that cause hindrance in the practice of yoga.

1. **Atyaahar:** Eating more than required, eating without being hungry and eating every now and then make up the condition of *atyaahar* or over-eating. This results in laziness, giddiness, excessive sleep, obesity and other physical ailments. Over-eating increases the effect of Tama Guna and leads to distraction.

2. **Prayas:** This means making an extra effort. An excess of physical and mental work exhausts the body and mind and acts as a hurdle in the practice of yoga.

3. **Prajalpa:** Talking incessantly about unimportant things is referred to as *prajalpa* in yoga. A waste of time, it is extremely distracting and results in confusion in the mind and disturbs concentration.

4. **Niyamgraha:** Engaging in activities that are not beneficial for yoga, like bathing in cold water on winter mornings and causing physical pain, is called Niyamgraha. This increases chances of the body suffering from ailments and causing hindrance to the practice of yoga.

5. **Jansang:** Interacting with people other than those interested in yoga is called *jansang*. A yoga practitioner gets entangled in worldly matters by *jansang* and develops feelings of love and hatred, envy, greed, possessiveness and anger. Hence, we should avoid *jansang* while practising yoga.

6.   **Chanchalta or laulyama:** A fickle mental state that prevents a person from concentrating on anything is referred to as chanchalta or laulyama. It gives rise to vices like greed and anger and distracts one from yoga.

ELEMENTS FACILITATING YOGA ACCORDING TO HATHYOG

The following excerpt is from *Hathyog Pradipika*:

Utsahatsahasadhhairyarttattvajyanachch nischayata
Janasamgaparityagat Shadbhiryogaha Prasidhhayati

This *sutra* means that enthusiasm, valour, patience, true knowledge, determination and avoiding public interaction help a person to achieve success in yoga.

1.   **Enthusiasm:** The feeling of happiness and interest shown towards a particular work before starting it is enthusiasm. An essential ingredient of success, enthusiasm makes the work easier and helps to complete it in time. An enthusiastic practitioner will derive benefit from yoga.

2.   **Valour:** There are three categories of people in the world. First, those who are scared to start a piece of work, in view of difficulties while doing it. Second, those who start the work, but abandon it midway when any problem or difficulty arises. Third, those who not only start the work but also complete it successfully, irrespective of difficulties. People belonging to the third category are called brave and valour is attributed to them. It is essential for a yoga practitioner to be brave because he often has to encounter difficulties while pursuing yoga.

3.   **Patience:** Not getting disturbed in times of distress is referred to as patience. It is essential for a person to be patient if he wants to practice yoga. Only such a person can practice yoga consistently and be successful.

4.   **True knowledge:** True knowledge of nature and the self are essential. True knowledge of things indicates the ability to perceive perpetual and non-perpetual matter in its true nature. When a yoga practitioner attains true knowledge, he is able to understand that the world is ephemeral. He is aware of the following: "I am not the body, and this *aatman* never dies. This world is full of suffering. The

main reason for my suffering is my attachment to this world." Developing a sense of detachment is philosophical knowledge in the true sense and leads to self-realization. Knowledge of the elements gives the practitioner knowledge of this true self.

5. **Determination:** When a person starts something, he should be determined to complete it successfully without abandoning it midway. Only a person with true determination can achieve success in yoga.

6. **Avoiding public interaction:** A true yoga practitioner should not interact with people who do not believe in yoga. By avoiding interaction, he avoids feelings of love and hate from clouding his mind. Interacting with others may make him vulnerable to ills like anger, possessiveness and greed, which will hinder the practice of yoga.
   A person can progress on the path of yoga by sincerely following the six guidelines described above.

ELEMENTS HINDERING YOGA ACCORDING TO PATANJALI YOG

The following *sutra* of Maharshi Patanjali describes elements hindering the practice of yoga:

Vyadhistyanashanshayapramadalasyaviratibhrantidarshanalabdha
Bhumikatvanavasthtithitvanichittavikshepastentarayaha

(Yog Sutra 1/30)

1. **Vyadhi (Sickness):** Fever caused due to imbalance in elements, juices and organs of the body is known as *vyadhi*. According to Ayurveda, imbalances of wind, bile and cough cause disorders in the body and improper digestion impedes the secretion of juices and elements essential for it. This causes *vyadhi*. Weakening of organs of the body is a symptom of *vyadhi*.

2. **Styaan (Langour):** Lack of mental energy to perform a certain activity is called *styaan*.

3. **Sanshaya (Doubt):** Uncertainties or anxieties like, "Would I be able to practise yoga?" or "Would I succeed?" are called *sanshaya*. They create mental confusion.

4. **Pramaad (Carelessness):** Not having enough motivation to practise yoga even when one has the physical ability and mental inclination to do it is called *pramaad*.

5. **Aalasya(Laziness):** Laziness to do something because of a sense of physical and mental heaviness is called a*alasya*. The body becomes heavy due to the attack of cough, while the mind seems heavy because of an excess of Tama Guna.

6. **Avirati (Addiction to objects):** Attachment with objects of desire or the lack of ascetic behaviour because of the wandering of sense organs is called *avirati*.

7. **Bhrantidarshan (Erroneous perception):** False or untrue knowledge and lack of belief in the yogic discipline is called *bhrantidarshan*.

8. **Alabdhabhumikatva (Failure to attain any stage of abstraction):** When a person is unable to reach the Samadhi stage even after constant practice of yoga, it is called *alabdhabhumikatva*.

9. **Anavasthhitatva (Instability):** Inability to keep the mind calm and to concentrate even after attaining the stage of Samadhi is called *anavasthhitatva*. The stage of Samadhi breaks even before one has reached one's goal.

ELEMENTS FACILITATING YOGA ACCORDING TO PATANJALI YOG

The following *sutra* from Patanjali's *Yog Sutra* describes the method of overcoming hindrances in the practice of yoga:

Tatpratishedharthamekatattvaabhyasaha

(*Yog Sutra* 1/32)

To remove hindrances and minor obstacles confronting the mind, you should practise the recollection of one elementary substance. This will enable you to concentrate totally and remove all hindrances and distractions. The best way to remove mental hindrances is to remember the Almighty.

Describing methods to remove mind-related disorders, *Yog Sutra* says:

Maitrikarunamuditopekshanamam
Sukhadukhapunyapunyavishayanam
Bhavanataschittaprasadanam

(*Yog Sutra* 1/33)

Through the practising of benevolence, compassion, complacency and disregard towards objects (that is persons who are respectively in possession) of happiness, grief, virtue and vice, the mind becomes purified.

1. **Maitri (Benevolence):** A yoga practitioner must be friendly with all happy people. He should refrain from harbouring feelings of envy, especially if the other person is wealthier than him. This feeling of benevolence will make him happy.

2. **Karuna (Compassion):** A yoga practitioner must be compassionate to a person who is in agony and reach out to those in distress. He should not isolate himself from the suffering of others or be overcome with feelings of hatred and selfishness. Compassion makes you happy.

3. **Mudita (Complacency):** Encountering a virtuous person should make a yoga practitioner happy. He should not doubt the integrity of such people and eschew feelings of envy or hatred.

4. **Upeksha (Indifference):** A yoga practitioner should avoid the company of vicious persons in order to steer away from vices like anger and violence. This is to ensure that these negative qualities do not have an impact on us.

THE FIVE PRANS

Pran is life, without which no person can live in this world. One can survive without water or food but cannot live without pran. Diffused throughout the body, pran controls its functions and keeps it healthy. **Pran Shakti** (energy of life) is responsible for an individual's various functions like sleeping, sitting, talking, running, thinking, eating and digestion. As long as pran shakti works properly, your body remains fit. In case of any imbalance, your body becomes ill. Pranayam has been included in yoga to organize and balance pran.

There is only one pran, but according to its activity, it has been divided into five parts:

1. **Pran:** It works in the body from the nose to the heart and regulates inhalation and exhalation. Pran Vayu or life force has two dimensions, *hakaar* and *sakaar*. Air is breathed out making the *hakaar* sound and breathed in making the *sakaar* sound. Considered the most important pran, it provides energy for the functioning of the respiratory and cardiac systems. Any irregularity in it causes disorders in them.

2. **Apaan:** The functioning of this pran extends from below the navel to your toes. It enables you to pass urine and stool. It aids in the delivery of babies and plays a role in ejaculation in males. Irregularity in apaan may cause gas, constipation, piles, diseases of urinary tract and sexual disorders.

3. **Samaan:** This pran functions from the heart to the navel and energizes every organ that lies in between,

namely, stomach, liver, kidney, pancreas etc. It generates hunger and helps to digest food. Any irregularity in Samaan Pran causes digestive disorders.

4. **Udaan:** Functioning between the throat and head, this pran keeps the neck, eyes, nose, ears and mouth active and keeps the working of the brain in order. The mind, pituitary and pineal glands derive energy from it. Udaan Pran coordinates activities like spitting, swallowing, speaking, hearing, smelling, tasting and contemplating. Any disorder in it may cause diseases of the eyes, ears, nose and throat, high blood pressure, stress, depression, loss of sleep, loss of memory, migraine, Alzheimer's disease, dyspepsia, Parkinson's disease and even insanity.

5. **Vyaan:** This pran is present and active in the entire body. It regulates flow of blood and energy to other prans and keeps them fit. It also cures disorders of the excretory system. Many diseases afflict the body when Vyaan Pran is not functioning well.

THE FIVE UPAPRAN
The five Upapran are as follows:
1. **Naag Vayu:** It makes hiccups and belching possible.

2. **Koorma Vayu:** It enables you to open and close your eyelids.

3. **Krikara:** It is responsible for hunger, thirst, sneeze and cough.

4. **Devadatta:** Sleep and yawning is caused by this vayu.

5. **Dhananjaya:** This vayu, which is pervasive in the body, creates Avyakta Naad. It remains in the body even after death and helps degenerate the body.

THE NAADI
An egg-shaped region between the navel and genitalia is the place of origin of 72,000 naadis (arteries, veins) and is called **Moolkand**. Out of these, 10 naadis are considered prominent. Of them, Idaa, Pingla and Sushumna Naadis are most important.

1. **Idaa Naadi:** Originating in Muladhar Chakra, this naadi goes up to the left nostril. As its nature is cool like the moon, it is also known as **Chandranaadi** or **Ganga** and is related to the nervous system. Its main function is to send the message of consciousness to all parts of the body. It also brings down the body's temperature. It not only cools down the body but also relaxes it and makes the mind inward looking. Negative energy flows through this naadi.

2. **Pingla Naadi:** This naadi originates in the right side of Muladhar Chakra and extends up to the right nostril. As its nature is hot like the sun, it is known as **Surya Naadi** or **Yamuna**. Related to the nervous system, it raises the body's temperature. Pingla Naadi prepares a person for rigorous labour and makes the mind outward looking. Physical labour is undertaken through this naadi and positive energy flows through it.

3. **Sushumna Naadi:** This naadi lies in the spinal cord and usually remains in a dormant state. It becomes active when energy flows through it. This happens when *Surya* and *Chandra Swar* start functioning. This state is called *sandhyakal* of naadis. When *swar* changes from chandra to surya, Sushumna Naadi is awakened for a few moments. In *Yog Shastra*, Sushumna Naadi is considered important as the kundalini power lies in a dormant state at the end of this naadi. It is also the abode of all those chakras and their powers that are usually dormant. A yoga practitioner purifies this naadi by enabling pran to flow through it. Regular practice leads to awakening of the kundalini power and chakras.

4. **Saraswati Naadi:** This naadi resides in the mouth.

5. **Gandhari Naadi:** This naadi flows up to the left eye.

6. **Hasthijihvaka Naadi:** This naadi flows up to the right eye.

7. **Poosha Naadi:** This naadi comes up to the left ear.

8. **Alamboosha Naadi:** This naadi comes up to the right ear.

9. **Kuhu Naadi:** This naadi flows up to the anus.

10. **Shankhini Naadi:** This naadi flows up to the genitalia.

PANCHKOSH

Panchkosh are five receptacles that keep the sensitivity of *aatman* intact. They keep *aatman* covered, hence the term *kosh*.

1. **Annamay Kosh:** According to *Taittiriya Upanishad*, the *aatman* of a living being is expressed in the form of food and juice. This is aatman's most prominent protective covering. An *annamaya sharir* (a body full of food and juice) is perceived as something that moves, does daily chores, and experiences happiness and sorrow. Because of this, worldly people suffer from the illusion that Annamaya Kosh is the *aatman*. But a body satiated with food is not *aatman*. The *aatman* only resides there.

   It is important for a yoga practitioner to ensure that the Annamaya Kosh remains clean. The food that one eats has the maximum impact on this kosh. Hence, our food should be simple, pure and easy to digest. Simultaneously, our body should be balanced, strong, supple and disease-free. It is also essential to keep our speech and sense organs under control. In yoga, Shatkarma and asanas are prescribed for cleansing Annamaya Kosh.

2. **Pranmay Kosh:** The five prans and ten organs present in the body are considered to be Pranmaya Kosh. The organs are also a medium of perceiving the aatman and regulating the body. In the absence of organs, the body will remain alive but will be incapable of feelings. The body's organs are empowered by pran. Though organs and pran apparently appear to be conscious, they are a receptacle of consciousness. They become conscious after contact with consciousness.

   It is essential for pranas present in the body to be healthy, empowered and organized so that this kosh remains clean. Disorganized pranas may lead to diseases. The main purpose of Pranayam is to cleanse this *kosh* and make it pure and supple. This results in improved respiration and health.

3. **Manonay Kosh:** Experiences of yoga practitioners have shown that the mind instructs organs of the body to perform their work. The mind stores experiences gained by these organs in Manonaya Kosh in the form of *sanskaras* (traits). Organs of the body are not independent, but are instruments of the mind. The five sense organs do not work simultaneously so the mind is unable to see anything it listens to or listen to anything it sees. This is why one doesn't even hear the sound of a passing train when one is engrossed in reading a book. Upanishads maintain that *aatman* is Manonaya but it is not *mann* (mind). The mind is also a *kosh* or receptacle of *aatman*.

A diseased mind causes a number of physical and mental ailments. Therefore, it is essential to keep the mind healthy and happy for effective practice of yoga. It is easier to control a healthy mind and divert it from material attractions. In yoga, Pratyahaar, Dharma and Naadanusandhan have been prescribed for controlling the mind.

4. **Vijnanmay Kosh:** The mind enables you to experience knowledge. Just as sense organs are controlled by the mind, the latter also works under instructions from the *aatman*. Questions have been raised in Kenopashad to determine what influences the mind to be attracted towards objects of desire and for eyes and pran to perform their function. It has been mentioned that the mind has its own mind, the eyes their own eyes, the speech its own speech, the pran its own pran and the ear its own ear. This is the *aatman*. A resolute person attains immortality by being acquainted with his aatman. The mind does not have access to *aatman* because it functions under its influence. The mind acts as an instrument of gathering knowledge and is motivated by aatman to do so. Experiences that the mind makes available to *aatman* make up what we call knowledge. Based on sense organs through which they are acquired, knowledge is classified into five categories: **Chakshu Vigyan** (knowledge acquired through vision), **Shotra Vigyan** (knowledge gained by hearing), **Graan Vigyan** (knowledge acquired by smelling), **Sparsh Vigyan** (knowledge gained by touching) and **Rasan Vigyan** (knowledge acquired by tasting).

    The reasoning ability of your mind should be resolute or you will be befuddled with doubts and will not be able to acquire any knowledge. Dhyaan or meditation has been prescribed for cleansing and invigorating Vijnanmaya Kosh. It improves your reasoning ability and helps you to take prudent decisions.

5. **Anandmay Kosh:** Acquiring knowledge is a blissful experience and motivates the mind, pran and *annamay sharir*. All living beings work in pursuit of happiness because of their aatman. In Brihadaranyak Upanishad, Sage Yajnavalkya tells his wife, Maitreyi, that aatman is the dearest of all things. It is only to provide happiness to the aatman that a husband is dear to his wife, a father dear to his son and wealth dear to the wealthy.

    It can be said that *anand* (bliss) is also a *kosh* (receptacle) of aatman; it is not aatman itself. All these *kosha*s envelop the aatman and appear to be filled with consciousness only through aatman. A person is usually able to experience bliss only for a brief period of time. As this bliss is transient, it continues only in the stage of Samaadhi. After a person attains sidhhi (perfection) in Samaadhi, all confusion and scepticism are resolved and feelings of love, hatred, passion, anger, greed, ego and possessiveness vanish. In the state of Samaadhi, a practitioner of yoga remains blissful. He has a feeling both of detachment and liberation.

SEVEN CHAKRAS

There are said to be 72,000 naadis (arteries and veins) that carry the life force in our body. Idaa, Pingla and Sushumna are three important naadis, of which Sushumna Naadi, or the central micro vessel, is of prime importance. It originates from the kandh sthan (area below the navel) and goes upward from the base of the spinal cord. Idaa and Pingla pass by its left and right side, respectively. Being very fine, these naadis appear like a cobweb and cannot be seen with the naked eye. They are radiant, pure and possess extraordinary powers. Many other naadis join these prominent naadis. Junctions or points where naadis meet are called pran or centre of life force. In yoga, they are called chakra, *kamal* or *padma*. There are seven chakras in the human body although some people are said to have experienced as many as eight chakras.

The seven chakras are — Muladhar, Svadhhisthan, Manipoor, Anaahat, Vishudhha, Ajnana and Sahasrar. These chakras are like lotus buds that have not blossomed. A yogi can help develop and make them blossom, using rigorous Chakra Saadhna. Although a yogi acquires extraordinary powers, he should not be distracted by these achievements. Undeterred, he should continue with his penance till he raises his kundalini power and attains liberation.

1. **Muladhar Chakra:** Known as the lowest chakra of energy or Brahmachakra, it is situated in Sushumna Naadi at the base of the spinal cord where the kundalini lies in a dormant stage. It controls and regulates reproductive organs and genitalia and is also connected to a person's power of smell. It is a lotus with four petals, with the syllables *vam*, *sham*, *shham* and *sam* marked. In karnika, the syllable *lam* is prithvibeej and is called *kulachakra* because the kundalini resides here. This chakra is related to element earth and the Annamaya Kosh. In all living beings, this chakra plays an important role in releasing Apaan Vaayu and facilitating release of faecal matter and urine, ejaculation and delivery of babies. Muladhar Chakra is also related to a person's subconscious mind from where the power of kundalini starts its journey towards Sahasrar Chakra. After rigorous practice, you can break Muladhar Chakra by making the downward-facing spiral kundalini look upwards. Thereafter, this power moves upwards from Sushumna Marg to Sahasrar Chakra where it interacts with Shiva. This process is called awakening of the kundalini power.

2. **Swadhhisthan Chakra:** Two inches above the Muladhar Chakra rests the Svadhhisthan Chakra. Sva means self and *adhhisthan* means place. When energy in this chakra starts functioning, a yoga practitioner is inclined to know his inner self. This chakra influences the reproductive organs and other related organs and is known to influence our ability to taste food.

Swadhhisthan Chakra, associated with a bright red lotus, has six petals. Syllables *bam, bham, mam, yam, ram* and *lam* are marked on each petal, respectively. Marked in karnika vam is jala beej mantra. This chakra, when empowered, affects a person's subconscious mind and attracts him towards sexual pleasures and food. Therefore, power should move ahead of this chakra. This chakra is also related to pranmaya kosh. The kundalini is awakened after rigorous practice, breaks Muladhar Chakra, and moves fast towards Swadhhisthan Chakra. In this stage, the practitioner attains *siddhi* (a supernormal perceptual state). When *shakti* is empowered in this chakra, one attains spontaneous knowledge of scriptures, becomes fearless and free from diseases. All living, earthly beings begin to get attracted towards such a practitioner.

3. **Manipoor Chakra:** Manipoor Chakra is also called Nabhi Chakra. *Mani* means precious stone and *poor* means town. Therefore, Manipoor also means 'town of precious stones'. It becomes radiant when a number of naadis converge there. It is believed that the element of fire is present in this chakra, which is related to the digestive system.

   Situated in the spinal cord behind the navel, this chakra consists of 10 petals marked with syllables *ddam, dham, nnam, tam, tham, dam, dhham, nam, pam* and *pham*. Agnibeej ram is marked in karnika. In this chakra, the spiral-shaped naadis are seen circulating five times like a snake. This chakra is like the young sun, being a storehouse of life force. It is related to life force, mobility, heat and production. Life force is its energy that helps in digestion and in carrying nutrients to various parts of the body. It is also a centre of Pranmaya Kosh. After rigorous practice, the vital energy moves upward from Muladhar Chakra and Swadhhisthan Chakra and reaches Manipoor Chakra. After reaching there, kundalini *shakti* is also called *madhyama shakti* because it has completed half the journey by the time it breaks Manipoor Chakra and reaches Sahasraar. By meditating at this stage, a practitioner attains many *siddhi*s (spiritual achievement) by meditating at this stage.

4. **Anaahat Chakra:** The word anaahat means unhurt. Situated near the heart in the Sushumna Naadi, **Anaahat Chakra** is also known as Hridaya Chakra. It is considered to be an important centre of microcosmic sound, which is known as **Anahad Naad**. This sound continuously resonates in our heart but is audible only when a practitioner reaches the highest state of Dhyaan. This *naad* can only be felt and not heard by the ears. Anaahat Chakra is the centre of pure feelings, love, peace and sensitiveness. It has 12 petals, with syllables *ka, kha, ga, gha, nna, ch, chh, ja, jh, yan, ta* and *th* marked on it. In the pericarp of the lotus is marked the vayu beej syllable *yam*. This chakra is related to the *manonaya kosh* (spiritual receptacle) that controls our feelings. In this chakra rests the life force in an ascending

position. This chakra also controls the heart and lungs. By continuous practice, a practitioner raises the kundalini power from Manipoor Chakra to Anaahat Chakra. He is in control of his sense organs and is assured of peace as all his desires and ego vanish.

5. **Vishudhhi Chakra:** This chakra is located in Sushumna, behind the throat, and is called **Shodhham Kendra** or purifying centre. It prevents the spread of toxic substances in the body. Yogic literature mentions ambrosia that is released from Sahasraar Chakra, reaches Vishudhhi Chakra, and from there is distributed to other organs. This flow of ambrosia increases the body's power, prowess, energy and longevity. If it is not controlled and regulated in this chakra, it moves to Manipoor Chakra and gets destroyed there. Vishudhhi Chakra is a lotus with 16 petals on which the syllables *a, aa, i, ee, u, oo, ri, iri, iri, iri, ay, ai, o, au, ang* and *ah* are marked. The aakash beej syllable *hum* is marked in the pericarp of the lotus. This chakra affects the neck, tonsils, sound-generating organ, thyroid and parathyroid glands. It is related to the Vijnanmaya Kosh, which is responsible for mental development. It also has the capacity to catch thought waves. By concentrating on this chakra, the mind becomes pure and serene. When a person raises his kundalini power from Anaahat Chakra and places it in Vishudhhi Chakra after vigorous practice, he attains several anaahat siddhis.

6. **Ajya Chakra:** This chakra is also called **Guru Chakra, Bhu Chakra** or **Madhyam Chakra** and is situated between two eyebrows. In the centre of this chakra lies **Gyan Netra** in the shape of a lamp's flame. Gyan Netra is also known as the **Third Eye, Shiva's Eye** or **Prajnaa Netra**. This is said to be a junction of Idaa, Pingla and Sushumna, representing Ganga, Yamuna and Saraswati, respectively. Hence, it is also called **Triveni** or **Sangam.** These three naadis meet at this chakra; this is called **Mukta Triveni.** It is a lotus with two petals on which the syllables *ham* and *ksham* are marked. The syllable *Aum* is marked in the pericarp of the lotus. Ajya Chakra is an abode of micro substances, mahattatva or pure conscience. It is also the centre of the mind and is considered to be an important point of higher conscience. Vyaan Vayu, an omnipresent power, lies in this chakra and is also related to Vigyanmaya Kosh. A yoga practitioner attains the stage of **Advaita** when the power of kundalini breaks Vishudhhi Chakra and reaches Ajya Chakra. Then, the mind stops wavering and concentrates solely on a single point.

7. **Sahasraar Chakra:** A lotus with a thousand petals, it is situated above Ajya Chakra and is also an abode of *jeevatma*. Here, energy meets Shiva and imparts spiritual bliss to a yoga practitioner. An epicentre of all powers, it is liberating in nature. This chakra has been described in various *shastras* by different names like Tenth Door, Nostril of Brahma, Nirvan Chakra, Upside Down Well and Date Palm Tree. Every

small naadi is related to this chakra. It is an important centre of high consciousness and is related to Anandmaya Kosh. Sahasraar in itself is not a chakra. It is a state reached by the practitioner when his conscious self merges with the *mahapran* (cosmic conscience). The practitioner reaches a higher state of *samaadhi* and starts knowing his inner self when the power of kundalini reaches Sahasraar. One who is engrossed in *saadhna* in this chakra is called *mukta* or emancipated.

NAADANUSANDHAN

In yoga, **Naadanusandhan** is considered to be the best method for keeping the mind well tuned and in rhythm. The unstruck sound, as it is best described, is heard in Naadanusandhan. A cosmic sound resonates in the universe, but cannot be heard by a person with a turbulent mind.

In the midst of broken and interrupted sounds, the only unstruck sound that is all pervading is that of *Aum* which is considered to be the symbolic sound of the Almighty. A research of this symbolic sound is called Naadanusandhan. Guru Gorakhnath and his disciples have taught about Naadanusandhan. The word naad is formed from two syllables *na* and *da*, meaning pran and fire, respectively. Naad originates from the union of pran and fire — the original elements of the world. Naad is their active form.

According to naad yogis, the first sound at the origin of the universe was *Aum*. The vibration of *Aum* led to the development of the universe. The *Aum* sound resonates and reverberates in the entire cosmos and is considered to be the sound symbol of the Almighty. It can be referred to as the origin of all sounds, words and sentences and as the music of the human spirit. *Aum*, like naad, is not a word in itself. It is a phenomenon you experience like the gurgling of a spring or the roaring of an aircraft. Just as sound is represented by the symbol of waves, there is a symbol for *Aum* as it cannot be written.

Naad can be divided into two types — Aahat Naad and Anahat Naad. Aahat naad (struck sound) is produced by vibrations of two or more objects or by striking musical instruments. It doesn't come into being on its own but it is created. It helps to keep the mind serene. Practitioners of this naad try to establish a communion with their favoured deity by playing bells, drums, cymbals and other musical instruments. These are tangible methods that practitioners use to enhance their mental concentration.

Anahat Naad is self-existent and divine. The sound produced either by one's conscience or by the contact of *brahma-randhra* (the opening at the top of the skull through which the soul is said to escape, for union with the absolute or death) with the divine power is the Anahat Naad. *Aum* is also Anahat Naad. When a person starts listening to the Anahat Naad, he attains a higher state of consciousness through Naadanusandhan.

Akash is the minutest of all Panchbhutas. Naad is a characteristic of Akash. As human beings are thinking beings, the world is considered to be the outcome of naad. A person without thought is lifeless because naad is the source of thought. All activities in the world are dependent on naad because naad represents the alphabet, alphabets make words, words make sentences and sentences gives rise to language.

Anahat Naad resides inside a practitioner. In this way, the Almighty makes His divine presence felt inside a practitioner. The Brahman is represented in the form of the word or sound. Therefore, naad is the search for Brahma in one's heart and is also called **Shabda Brahma**. Just as a mahout controls a frenzied elephant with the help of his hook, Anahat Naad controls a frenzied mind.

For this, close your ears with your two thumbs, eyes with two index fingers and nose and mouth with the middle fingers and acquire the Muktaasan posture. Now, try to listen to the naad of the right ear in Shambhari Mudra. The external sounds/noise stops going into the ears when the mind is concentrated on the naad. The practitioner is able to overcome his mental turmoil and attains peace after regular practice of naad for 15 days.

In the initial stages of Naadanusandhan, the practitioner hears many types of sounds like roaring of seas and wind. But through constant practice, the volume of the sound gets reduced. During the middle stage of practice, when the life force becomes stable in Sushumna, the sound resembles that of conch and bell. When the life force becomes stable in Brahma-randhra, the practitioner hears sound that resemble that of a flute, veena or any tinkling ornament.

A yogi should contemplate upon even the minutest of sounds. A *yogi* forgets everything and become engrossed in Samadhi when his mind mingles with the naad. Thus, the mind's natural tendencies get restricted/reduced automatically when it concentrates on naad. The *kundalini* power awakes and becomes more vigorous by Naadanusandhan. When it breaks the seven Chakras, establishes communion with Shiva, the practitioner is liberated.

SWAR YOG

Swar doesn't refer to the air coming in and going out of our nostrils. It is related to the *pran*, which is an important part of respiration. A person breathes uninterruptedly throughout his life without even being conscious of it. In fact, breathing is our only possession because the moment we lose it, we cease to exist.

In Yog Shastra, the flow of energy is called naadi. Three kinds of flow occur in our nose from time to time — Idaa, Pingla and Sushumna. When you breathe through the left nostril, it is called the flow of Idaa Naadi. When you breathe through the right nostril, it is called the flow of Pingla Naadi. When we breathe from both nostrils simultaneously, it is called the flow of Sushumna Naadi.

Describing Hathyog, Guru Gorakhnath has pointed to the conjugation of syllables *ha* (the power of the sun or the flow of Pingla Naadi) and *tha* (the power of the moon or the flow of the Idaa Naadi). Accordingly, Hathyog is the procedure required for harmony of *Surya* and *Chandra swar*s, by which *pran* is able to flow in the sushumna mode. Thus, with Hathyog one can attain the higher state of mind by practising proper breathing.

When you breathe through the left nostril, your cerebral activities get a boost. When your right nostril is active, there is an increase in physical activities. You are inclined towards spiritual activity when breathing takes place uniformly through both nostrils. Thus, we know what kind of activities we should engage in, depending on the nature of breathing. If we breathe through the right nostril during dhyan, our body and mind get restless. Similarly, the mind becomes extremely fickle when we breathe through the left nostril. When both nostrils are active, our mental concentration improves. This is why in yoga, Pranayam is recommended before dhyan as Pranayam enables the flow of *swar* to Sushumna Naadi that facilitates dhyan.

To know which nostril is active at a particular time, put one of your fingers just outside the nostrils and breathe forcefully. Do rechak slightly forcefully and you will automatically know which nostril is involved in inhalation or exhalation. *Swar Shastra* states that a person should breathe in the *surya swar* at night and the *chandra swar* during the day. This ensures that the body remains healthy.

According to *Shiva Swarodaya*, Shastra Swar remains in a naadi for 2½ ghadis (one ghadi is equal to 24 minutes, hence 2½ ghadis is equal to one hour). Thereafter, it starts flowing in the other nostril. The period of transition is called *sandhyakal* and lasts for one to four minutes. This has also been substantiated by science that says that one hemisphere of our brain remains active for 1 to 1½ hours. After this, energy is transferred from one hemisphere of the brain to the other by the corpus callosum, which is a broad band of nerve fibres joining the two hemispheres of the brain. This process takes anything from one to four minutes to complete.

The inhalation and exhalation of a person who is physically weak takes longer than that of a normal person. According to Swarodaya Shastra, the energy being restored in the body is inversely proportional to the length of breathing. As a result of this energy, the practitioner attains several mental and pranic abilities.

On the other hand, the body expands or consumes more energy if the duration of breathing is longer and also becomes weak. Hence, a yogi should ensure that the length of breathing becomes longer except during Pranayam. According to *Swar Vigyan*, if a person feels that he is falling ill, he should change his *swar* or breathing pattern. A change in breathing pattern often helps in the critical stages of diseases. *Swar Yog* describes different breathing patterns for different diseases and activities. For example, breathing by Pingla Naadi or *surya swar* is recommended during the following activities: eating, exercise, physical labour, studying, teaching, excreting and during delivery of babies. Similarly, breathing by Idaa Naadi or *chandra swar* is recommended for the following activities: drinking milk, snacking, urinating, going on a pilgrimage, entering home, taking medicines and doing auspicious work. While performing yoga, prayer, dhyaan and satsang, breathing by Sushumna Naadi or the middle sound is prescribed.

Perform the following activities to change the breathing pattern:
- Concentrate on the current breathing pattern.
- Lie on the side opposite to the nostril from which you want to breathe.
- Block the movement of air of the opposite nostril by stuffing cotton.
- Inhale the maximum through the active nostril and exhale through the other nostril.
- Running, physical labour and Pranayam are helpful in changing the breathing pattern.